D1339697

Please renew or return it .... date
shown on your receipt

www.hertsdirect.org/libraries

Renewals and enquiries: 0300 123 4049
Textphone for hearing or   0300 123 4041
speech impaired users:

L32

Hertfordshire

Lady Blessington at Naples

Lady Blessington at Naples

EDITED BY

Edith Clay

Introduction by Sir Harold Acton

Hamish Hamilton: *London*

First published in Great Britain 1979
by Hamish Hamilton Limited
Garden House, 57–59 Long Acre, London WC2E 9JL

Copyright © 1979 by Edith Clay

British Library Cataloguing in Publication Data

Blessington, Marguerite Gardner, *Countess of*
 Lady Blessington at Naples.
 1. Naples – Social life and customs
 I. Title II. Clay, Edith
 945'.73   DG845.6

 ISBN 0–241–89975–3

Phototypeset by Western Printing Services Ltd, Bristol
Printed and bound in Great Britain by
Redwood Burn, Trowbridge and Esher.

Contents

List of Illustrations

Acknowledgements

I am deeply indebted to Sir Harold Acton for having written the *Introduction* to this book and for having given me valuable advice in its editing, and to Mr. Raleigh Trevelyan for his encouragement and counsel.

I also wish to express my thanks to the following persons at Naples: Professor Raffaello Causa, Director of the National Gallery at Capodimonte; Signor Calcagno of the National Library, and Maestro Ernesto Rocco, owner of the Villa Belvedere.

As regards the illustrations, I am indebted to the authorities of the Victoria and Albert Museum and Wallace Collection, London; and of the National Museums at Capodimonte and San Martino at Naples, also to Mr. Ivo Pakenham and to Miss Jane Flower who has kindly given me permission to reproduce her drawing of the Archbishop of Taranto by Count d'Orsay.

The map on page 24 is from *Naples and Campania Revisited* by Edward Hutton, Hollis & Carter, London 1958.

I would like to record my gratitude to Miss Letitia Thomas who not only typed out the manuscript of this book, but my previous three as well.

"Genius may be said to reside in an illuminated palace of crystal, unapproachable to other men, which, while it displays the brightness of its inhabitants, renders also any blemishes in her form more visible by the surrounding light, while men of ordinary minds dwell in opaque residences, in which no ray of brightness displays the faults of ignoble mediocrity."

(Lady Blessington – *Stray Thoughts*)

". . . and above all women of her time she fascinated, and fascination is a moral grace, for it has its source in the soul."

(Lady Wilde on Lady Blessington.
Dublin University Magazine, March 1855)

Ah! Not alone the lovely face,
The lovely heart is there,
The smile that seems to light and win,
Speaks of the deeper world within.'

(Poem to Lady Blessington
by Letitia Elizabeth Landon)

Introduction and Preface

Introduction

Miss Edith Clay has already introduced us to the delightful ramblings of *Ramage in South Italy:* and more recently her erudite and entertaining *Sir William Gell in Italy.Letters to the Society of Dilettanti, 1831–1835.* Once again she returns to the incomparable Bay and we are indebted to her for reviving the Neapolitan journals of Lady Blessington, a beauty in perfect harmony with her surroundings.

In 1817 Stendhal remarked that Naples was "the only capital in Italy": all the other large cities reminded him of Lyons. This was true until the exit of the Bourbons, and until the nineteenth century most visitors were equipped with sufficient knowledge of the classics to enjoy Naples not only as a capital in a situation of magical enchantment but also as a place which brought ancient history and legend to life. Besides Pompeii and Herculaneum, Virgil's tomb attracted hundreds of pilgrims. More has been excavated since, but the ruins were less ruined than now, as can be seen from the old engravings. Even the gestures of the population could be traced to remote antiquity as in Canon De Jorio's ingenious study *La Mimica degli Antichi investigata nel gestire Napoletano* (1832).

A city so uniquely spectacular inspired many foreigners to record their impressions. Among those which were published Lady Blessington's afford us a more intimate and accurate view of the local society as well as of the famous sights described previously by Henry Swinburne, Eustace and other erudite wanderers. Instead of the three hectic days of the average modern tourist Lady Blessington spent almost three years there.

After a miserable childhood and marriage, at the age of fifteen, to a sadistic monster, Lady Blessington had been lifted into the lap of exotic luxury by her second husband and she was determined to make the most of it. Lord Blessington was an inflated type of the *milordo inglese*, extravagant, wayward and hospitable;

and he had chosen the right person to organize his existence in a civilized manner – an Irish beauty endowed with intelligence. The youthful Count d'Orsay had so bewitched this singular couple that they were to form a happy *ménage à trois*. The French dandy's flamboyance appealed to that of the middle-aged peer: Lord Blessington was infatuated with a Narcissus too fond of himself to love others. Michael Sadleir infers that d'Orsay was impotent: be that as it may, Lady Blessington's affection for him was that of an over-indulgent mother, for her physical temperament had been chilled by her former marriage. Mary Ann Power, her youngest sister, described as a primrose by the side of a peach-blossom, and Charles Mathews, a budding architect who shared his host's *penchant* for miming, were other members of the house party assembled on the Vomero hill, then sprawling with gay country houses, private gardens and orchards, now almost a separate city.

The spacious mansion which Lady Blessington calls the Palazzo Belvedere in her nostalgic account of its amenities was ideally suited to so bountiful a hostess. It is clearly depicted in the background of Angelica Kauffmann's portrait of a former Prince of Belvedere, painted in 1782, exhibited in the gallery of Capodimonte. Oddly enough Lady Blessington does not mention that it had been a favourite residence of Queen Maria Carolina during the hot weather. Twice a week through May and October the grounds had then been open to the public, which could watch various sports and games or listen to music in the open air theatre "formed of trees and plants, the proscenium elevated and of verdant turf, and the seats of marble." The garden adjoined the neo-classical Villa Floridiana, now a public museum housing the Duke of Martina's art collection, which the elderly King had given to his morganatic spouse, the dumpy Sicilian Duchess of Floridia.

Lady Blessington's spelling of Neapolitan names is erratic but her descriptions of royal residences when they were pullulating with life are eloquently evocative. Therein lies their value for us who visit Naples today. She enables us to visualize conditions at the end of Ferdinand I's long reign, so gloomily described by others. Though her friendship with d'Orsay, the son of a Bonapartist general, inclined her to sympathize with Murat's régime and those who had served it, she was fair to old Ferdinand and less biased than her compatriot Lady Morgan, who had frequented the same society in 1820. But Lady Morgan had spent a relatively short time in Naples, scribbling copious notes on the wing. The resulting tomes on Italy were evidently compiled in a hurry. Her saltiest anecdotes are embedded in footnotes instead of being woven into the text. For instance, remarking that the Neapolitan Court was closed during Lent when the King, to show his piety, "passed the days in hunting boars instead of receiving them," she adds in a footnote: "The King never goes forth for the chase without arming himself with a heron's foot: which he places in his button-hole, as the most effective charm against the *Monacello* (the Neapolitan hobgoblin), or against the ill-luck of meeting an old woman or a priest, as he crosses the threshold – both ill omens for the day! When Lord XXX came to an audience to take leave of his Majesty on his return to England, the King told him he had a little *bouquet d'adieu* for him; and when his lordship probably dreamed of a gold snuff-box with the royal face set round with brilliants on the lid, he was presented with the heron's foot, as a spell against all accidents in an English fox-chase, and a remembrance of royal friendship and Neapolitan field sports."

Lady Blessington, on the other hand, revised her journals carefully some twelve years after her residence at Naples. She had always written for pleasure, but now she wrote to increase her diminished income as well. Instead of repining at her loss of fortune she relived the golden past with philosophy and humour. As she never referred to her husband or d'Orsay by name we must glean further particulars from the letters of her guest Charles Mathews. "In one corner of the large saloon," he wrote from Belvedere to his mother, "stood Lady Blessington's table, laden with books and writings; Count d'Orsay's in another, equally adorned with literary and artistic litter, Miss Power's and mine completed the arrangement, while Lord Blessington strolled and chatted from one to the other, and then dived into his own sanctum, where he divided his time between fresh architectural schemes for his castle in the air and the novel *de Vavasour* on which he was busily engaged." Lord Blessington had bought Byron's commodious yacht the *Bolivar*, so that his party could vary their excursions by sea and land. Their sightseeing was arranged on a lavish scale with excellent meals provided in unlikely places.

"A collation that would not have shamed the Sybaritic inhabit-

ants said to have once possessed Paestum was spread in the
temple of Neptune." This was followed by "a highly intellectual
treat, as Mr. George Howard (later Lord Morpeth) complied with
the pressing request of the company to recite a poem, written by
him when at college, on the ruins we were then contemplating.
The poem was admirable, and so spirited as to convey an impression that it must have been written on the spot, and under the
inspiration which the actual scene, and not merely a classical
description of it, had created." At Pompeii the learned Sir William Gell, who was such a martyr to gout that he had to be carried
in a litter, acted as their indomitable guide. Here another *recherché*
collation was served and Sir William "asserted that Pompeii
never before saw so delicious a *déjeuner à la fourchette.*"

Lady Blessington wrote with such relish about cooking that she
had to drop into French. No doubt her chef was an artist but one
feels sorry for the goldfinch which he had caged "in a temple of
spun sugar, as an ornament for the centre of the table for the third
course; and the poor bird, while the *convives* were doing honour
to the *entremets* and *sucreries*, fluttered through the temple and
beat his wings against its sugary pillars, till they were encrusted
with its clammy substance."

The Villa Belvedere was essentially a summer retreat, and after
one winter in its draughty halls the luxurious Blessingtons
moved into the cosier Villa Gallo at Capodimonte which
belonged to the retired ambassador of that name. Don Marzio
Mastrilli, Marquis of Gallo, had been a petted protégé of Queen
Maria Carolina to whom he owed his advancement, but he
turned against her in adversity and Murat created him a duke –
though Napoleon had a low opinion of his merit. He was a
courtier rather than a diplomatist. Fortunately he disregarded
Maria Carolina's request to destroy her indiscreet letters to him,
for they help to explain her difficult character. He had entered
upon his anecdotage when Lady Blessington became his tenant.
The house had been designed for him by Antonio Niccolini, the
architect of the Villa Floridiana, and the Murats had often stayed
there. Gallo's heirs sold it to Count del Balzo, Ferdinand II's
gentleman-in-waiting, who married the mature Queen Mother
Maria Isabella. Most of the pleasure grounds have since been
converted into vineyards and orchards.

It is noticeable that many of the Blessingtons' Neapolitan
friends were under a temporary cloud owing to their past

allegiance to Kings Joseph Bonaparte and Murat, but Filangieri, Florestano Pepe, and Ischitella in particular were to play important rôles during the reign of Ferdinand II when they were reinstated.[1] On an eminence far from lonely sat Giuseppe Capecelatro, the Archbishop of Taranto to whom Croce has devoted a perceptive essay.[2] Born in 1744, he had been consecrated archbishop at the age of thirty-four but the political whirlwind had swept him back to Naples at the turn of the century, where he remained a brilliant lodestar for all the itinerant celebrities until his death at the age of ninety-two in 1836. As Prince Henry of Prussia remarked on meeting him: "When you come to Naples you must see Pompeii, Vesuvius and the Archbishop of Taranto."

An enlightened survivor of the *ancien régime*, he also appealed to the restless romantics of a younger generation, such as Madame de Staël and Lamartine. Princes, poets, artists and scientists corresponded with him, and all who met him were charmed by his serene personality and impressed by his diffuse erudition. Among others Lady Morgan has portrayed him in her *Italy* as "one of the finest illustrations of benignity that Nature, in her happiest mood, ever struck off to reconcile man to his species. . . . Still attached, with all the enthusiasm of youth, to letters and science, his mornings are given up to his books, his medals, and his engraved gems; his early and hospitable dinnertable is seldom without some polished or literary guest, and his afternoons and evenings are devoted to successive circles of friends (whom habits of long and reverential attachment congregate round him) and to some few well-recommended foreigners who, in the desire of knowing one of the most celebrated characters in Italy, solicit permission to attend his *prima sera*." In those days, to paraphrase Virginia Woolf, it was easier than now for people to stand on an eminence which they scarcely struggled to keep, but enjoyed by unanimous consent.

Lady Morgan mentions with approbation that he had written "to prove that the celibacy of the clergy was a crime against nature and good morals". He also wrote against the Jesuits, the persecution of authors, and the claustration of nuns in convents;

---

[1] See Harold Acton: *The Last Bourbons of Naples*.

[2] See Benedetto Croce: *Uomini e Cose della Vecchia Italia, Serie Seconda*, Bari, 1927.

and he framed a new set of rules for the seminary of Taranto (in 1789) to discourage abstract speculation on pre-destination and original sin and encourage the teaching of agricultural methods so that country priests might enlighten their peasant parishioners. He even thought seminarists should be instructed in surgery and obstetrics to assist poor women in labour. His hobbies range from numismatics to Polish literature: in fact he was an amiably broad-minded dilettante and probably no more of a sceptic than Cardinal de Bernis and other contemporary prelates who cultivated the society of clever people. Lady Blessington, who was to win fame as a London hostess, regarded the Archbishop as a model host, "whose urbanity smooths the asperities of national prejudices, and whose tact leads the conversation to subjects of general interest".

The society and many of the scenes she described with such zest have vanished, but the Neapolitan people remain and those who really know them will agree with her estimate of their honesty, their politeness free from servility, and their good humour free from coarseness or boisterousness. "The more I see of the Neapolitans, the better I like them," she declared. And she paid unconscious tribute to the reigning Bourbon: "We are told that the Italians writhe under the despotism of their rulers; but nowhere have I seen such happy faces." It might be objected that her ladyship, as a specially privileged onlooker, was superficial in her judgements of "the good peasants who inhabit the lower part of Belvedere", but she had more opportunities to observe them than the modern flitter-by. Moreover it is clear that she was *simpatica* to the Neapolitans: no amount of wealth could compensate for the supercilious airs of distant superiority assumed by many foreigners. Her vivacity and good nature permeate *The Idler in Italy* and keep it fresh today.

Harold Acton

Preface

My reasons for bringing out this book are twofold. Firstly, I believe Lady Blessington to be a much maligned woman; extravagant, misguided and indiscreet as her actions may sometimes have been. Much has been written about the remarkable association between Lord and Lady Blessington and Count Alfred d'Orsay; and since scandal seems to appeal to the world in general, this is the prevailing impression regarding these personages. I hope that the brief account of Lady Blessington's life, which appears as *Appendix A*, may put her character into better perspective and cause people to think of her in a more favourable light, in spite of the role she must have played in helping to bring about the outrageous marriage between her step-daughter and d'Orsay. Indeed, Forster writing of Lady Blessington in his *Life of Walter Savage Landor* says that she was "enchanting, carefree and irresistibly charming – exceptionally true and affectionate-hearted".

Landor was a great friend and admirer of Lady Blessington. When Lady Blessington was staying at Florence in 1826, she took his daughter, Julia, and his son, Walter, into her care when their mother had malignant fever.[1] Another instance of her kindness was when she took Henry Fox to stay at her villa at Naples after he had injured his back. Landor never believed that d'Orsay was Lady Blessington's lover and he constantly stayed at Gore House after her return to London. Henry Fothergill Chorley, the art and music critic, wrote on 7 May 1838 of "a dinner at Kensington *tête-à-tête* with Lady Blessington and Mr. Landor, she talked her best, brilliant and kindly, and without that touch of self-consciousness which she sometimes displayes (sic) when worked up to by flatterers and gay companions".[2]

---

[1] *Savage Landor* by Malcolm Elwin, London, 1941, p. 237.

[2] *Op. cit.*, p. 330.

Sir Walter Besant remarked, "there must have been something singularly attractive about her manners and conversation. It is not a stupid person or an unattractive woman that such success as hers was attained",[1] and Mrs. Newton Crosland (well-known in London Society) wrote "in all my intercourse with Lady Blessington I cannot recall a word from her lips which conveyed an idea of laxity of morals, while very often her advice was excellent. She was always in a high degree generously sympathetic with the struggling and unfortunate; not in words only but in actions, for she would take a great deal of trouble to do a small service, and was a kind friend to many who were shy of acknowledging their obligation." I believe that Lady Blessington did not deserve the havoc, financial and moral which devotion to d'Orsay made of her life. She must have been a fascinating woman. We cannot see the irresistible smile, or hear the voice or laugh which entranced her friends, and ensured forgiveness for the most maddening faults. But we have to believe that it was so. Secondly, Lady Blessington's account of her residence at Naples will, I believe, give pleasure and enjoyment to all those who know and love that city and its surroundings.

Marguerite Countess of Blessington was approaching her thirty-fifth birthday when she arrived at Naples and had been married to the Earl of Blessington for five years. They resided at Naples from 17 July 1823 until sometime in February 1826 and Lady Blessington's Neapolitan Journals cover this period of time. She gives an account of her travels in *The Idler in Italy* which was published in two volumes in 1839 by Baudry's European Library, Paris and the journals printed in this book appear in Vol. ii, pp. 188–470. She obviously wrote very full accounts of her activities in her day-to-day diaries, but when she came to prepare *The Idler in Italy* some years after her return to England, although at first the entries follow each other more or less consecutively, later there are long lapses of time with the barest indications of date. I have endeavoured to make the dating as clear as possible in this abridged edition. Lady Blessington included her poems *To Pompeii* and *Lines on the Death of Lord Byron*: I have printed these as *Appendix B*.

The Idler in Italy has not, I think, ever been republished, although later writers have quoted from it. She is often inaccurate

[1] *Fifty Years Ago*, London, 1888, p. 205.

and inconsistent in her usage of titles. For instance, an Italian duke and duchess are given their titles in the French style – I have not altered these in the text, but have, where possible, given identifying footnotes. Like Queen Victoria, Lady Blessington frequently underlined words to give added emphasis.

Shortly after the publication of Lady Blessington's book, T. Uwins, the artist, wrote to her from London on 3 April 1839, "May I be allowed, without charge of impertinence, to tell your Ladyship how much delight I am getting from *The Idler in Italy*. To hear tell of scenes and characters so well known to me, and to follow your ladyship's discriminating pen through delineations as faithful as they are interesting, is a pleasure that none can envy more than your humble servant. Year after year, since my return from those delightful regions, I have been looking for such a book from Lady Blessington; the delay, perhaps judicious – at any rate, the book loses none of its freshness, and in many cases, may even be read with additional zest derived from the lapse of time. Like everything done by your ladyship, it seems to appear exactly at the proper moment;" and in *Ramage in South Italy*, I have remarked that she was "a brilliant and thought-provoking writer and gives a vivid account of the circle in which she moved at Naples. Some of her writings show a more serious and deeply-interesting side of her character." Lady Blessington had a strong sense of humour, although touched by a peculiar turn of grave irony.

Shortly after their arrival at Naples, Lord and Lady Blessington, Count d'Orsay and Lady Blessington's youngest sister, Miss Mary Ann Power, took up residence in the Palazzo Belvedere (now Villa) on the Vomero: later on they moved to the Villa Gallo at Capodimonte. The young architect, Charles James Mathews, whom Lord Blessington had employed in connection with rebuilding projects on his Irish estates, also lived with them for part of the time. Madden remarks of him that "a merrier man within the limits of becoming mirth it would be difficult to find . . . he was an admirable mimic and fond of fun and frolic".

On 13 November 1823 Mathews writes, "What words can adequately describe the Paradise to which I was introduced to Naples! The Palazzo Belvedere, situated about a mile and a half from the town on the heights of Vomero, overlooking the city, and the beautiful turquoise-coloured bay dotted with latine sails, with Vesuvius on the left, the island of Capri on the right, and the lovely coast of Sorrento stretched out in front, presented an enchanting scene. The house was the perfection of an Italian palace, with its exquisite frescoes, marble arcades, and succession of terraces one beneath the other, adorned with hanging groves of orange trees and pomegranates shaking their odours among festoons of vines and luxuriant creepers, affording agreeable shade from the noonday sun, made brighter by the brilliant parterres of glowing flowers, while refreshing fountains splashed in every direction among statues and vases innumerable. I was naturally entranced, and commenced a new existence."

Lady Blessington, then in her zenith, and certainly one of the most beautiful as well as one of the most fascinating women of her time, formed the centre figure in the little family group assembled within its precincts.

Count d'Orsay, then a youth of nineteen, was the next object of attraction, and I have no hesitation in asserting was the *beau ideal* of manly dignity and grace. He had not yet assumed the marked peculiarities of dress and deportment which the sophistications of London life subsequently developed. He was the model of all that could be conceived of noble demeanour and youthful candour; handsome beyond all question, accomplished to the last degree; highly educated, and of great literary acquirement; with a gaiety of heart and cheerfulness of mind that spread happiness on all around him. His conversation was brilliant and engaging, as well as clever and instructive – He was, moreover, the best fencer, dancer, swimmer, runner, dresser; the best shot, the best horseman, the best draughtsman of his age. Possessed of every attribute that could render his society desirable, I am sure I do not go too far in pronouncing him the perfection of a youthful nobleman.

Then came Miss Power, Lady Blessington's younger sister, somewhat demure in aspect, of quiet and retiring manners, contrasting sweetly with the more dazzling qualities which sparkled around her. Lady Blessington has been described as a peach blossom, and Miss Power as a primrose beside her.

This formed the family party, and I soon found it as fully devoted to mental cultivation and the prosecution of literary pursuits, as to the more natural occupations of pleasure and enjoyment.

The house was the *rendezvous* of all the *literati* of the place, and the point of attraction of all the English visitors of distinction who were so frequently passing through it . . .[1] On 24 March 1824 he describes to his Mother their mode of life:

". . . In the morning we generally rise from our beds, couches, floors, or whatever we happen to have been reposing on upon the night before, and those who have morning-gowns and slippers put them on as soon as they are up. We then commence the ceremony of washing, which is longer or shorter in its duration, according to the taste of the persons who use it. You will be glad to know that from the moment Lady Blessington awakes she takes exactly one hour and a half to the time she makes her appearance, when we usually breakfast; this presience is remarkably agreeable, as we cannot always calculate thus upon the possible time of our breakfasting, there is sometimes a difference of five or six minutes, but seldom more. This meal taking place latish in the day, I always have a premature breakfast in my own room the instant I am up, which prevents my feeling that hunger so natural to the human frame from long fasting. After our collation, if it be fine, we set off to see the sights, walks, palaces, monasteries, views, galleries of pictures, antiquities, and all that sort of thing; if rainy, we set to our drawing, writing, reading, billiards, fencing, and everything in the world. At dinner we generally contrive to lay in a stock of viands that may last us through the evening, and sometimes succeed.

In the evening each person arranges himself (or herself) at his table and follows his own concerns till about ten o'clock, when we sometimes play whist, sometimes talk, and are always delightful! About half-past eleven we retire with our flat candlesticks in our hands, after wishing each other the compliments of the season and health to wear it out. Thursdays usually, and Sundays, the Italian master comes, though for the present we have dropped him.

At dinner Lady Blessington takes the head of the table, Lord Blessington on her left, Count d'Orsay on her right, and I at the bottom. We have generally for the first service a joint and five *entrées*; for the second, a *roti* and five *entrées*, including sweet things."[2]

[1] *Life of Charles James Mathews, edited by Charles Dickens*, London, Macmillan, 1879, vol. i, pp. 92–5.
[2] *Op. cit.*, vol. i, pp. 146–7.

Three months later he gives a romantic description of the effect of moonlight from the palazzo Belvedere:

"The sea air is always fresh, and the terraces always cool, admitting of most enchanting walks by the light of the moon; indeed nothing can equal these terraces overlooking the bay, and perfumed with the exquisite fragrance of the flowers below. An Italian moonlight also differs materially from ours in England from the total absence of all fog, or damp mists; not even the slightest dew is perceptible. Not a breath of air is stirring or a sound of any kind to be heard except the exquisite melody of our darling nightingales, who, from the groves above which we stand and in which we are enveloped, burst forth at short intervals with all that brilliancy and richness so often celebrated, but, in such perfection, so seldom heard. Belvedere, at this hour, is elevated into the very highest heaven of poetry. Every moonlight scene that ever was described is here realised and surpassed. The glorious combination of sea, mountain, and island, under the soothing gentle light of the chaste Diana, is viewed with a feeling of reverent admiration that absolutely inspires the soul with an unearthly delight. The perfect clearness with which every object is visible is quite inconceivable. In the midst of the glistening reflection of the light on the glassy surface of the sea, is frequently seen the small white sail of the fishing boat gliding in silence through the calm water, or the shining gondola enjoying the heavenly scene, trailing after it a long line of silvery brightness, and sometimes the subdued sounds of their music falling upon the ear. It is really enchanting, and each night, with various effects of light, I enjoy it from the terrace, which adjoins my bedroom, when all the rest of the house are quietly asleep. Here I literally sit for hours in my morning-gown, without the least desire to sleep, watching with delighted eye the fireflies, their golden wings glistening as they chase each other from place to place, and sometimes quite illuminating by their numbers the deep purple shade of the garden.[1]

The Blessingtons soon formed a large circle of friends, both of Neapolitans, English residents and visitors to Naples. Among the most faithful of these was the classical topographer and antiquary, Sir William Gell,[2] to whom Lady Blessington often

[1] *Op. cit.*, vol. i, pp. 153–4.
[2] See *Sir William Gell in Italy. Letters to the Society of Dilettanti 1831–1835*

refers in her journals. Gell had travelled widely in Greece and Turkey, and had led the Society of Dilettanti's second expedition to Ionia in 1811–1813. He and his friend the Hon. Keppel Craven had been Chamberlains to Caroline Princess of Wales, and for some years prior to 1820, Gell had shared a Gothic villa constructed in the ruins of Domitian's Palace on the Palatine Hill at Rome with Charles Mills. From 1820 until his death there in 1836, Gell resided at Naples. From an early age he had suffered from gout, and from the time he went to Naples, he was so severely crippled by it that he had to be carried about in a chair. Nevertheless, he managed to act as *cicerone*, not only to Lady Blessington but to many English visitors (including Sir Walter Scott) conducting them round the neighbouring classical sites. He wrote many learned books on his travels including *Pompeiana* (illustrated by himself) which went into several editions. As well as being renowned for his scholarship and learning, Gell was also very amusing and witty. Mathews writes of him, ". . . and dear old, kind, gay Sir William Gell, who while wheeling himself about the room in his chair, for he was unable to walk a step without help, alternatively kept his friends on the broad grin with his whimsical sallies and droll anecdotes, and instructed them from the stores of his wonderful archaeological knowledge and practical experience, always as pleased and ready to impart his instructive information as they were to receive it – at one moment playing on a rough Greek double flute to his dog (who was an accomplished singer) with as much gravity as if really accompanying a celebrated *virtuoso*, and the next turning over endless portfolios, and illustrating their treasures by *viva voce* comments. His talent for rapid sketching was remarkable, and the accuracy with which he could put upon paper from memory anything he had casually seen was most extraordinary, his drawings bearing minute comparison afterwards with the objects themselves."[1]

A good example of Gell's whimsical manner of writing is given in the following letter which he wrote to Lady Blessington sometime in 1824 proposing an excursion to Pompeii; "I have to inform your ladyship that the weather seemingly consenting to relent, Dr. Watson (medical attendant on Sir William Drummond and

---

edited by Edith Clay in collaboration with Martin Frederiksen, London, Hamish Hamilton, 1976.

[1] *Op. cit.*, vol. i, pp. 102–3.

one of the most eminent linguists of his time in Europe) and I have an idea of a trip to Pompeii tomorrow, and having had a sort of half agreement with your amiable party, I think perhaps you may not be disinclined for the excursion.

Suppose we say we will meet there at or about twelve, and bring our dinners in our pockets, and dine either in the quarters at the great table, or any where else about three or four, for later it may be cold, but about three will be very agreeable, the place being sunny or sheltered. You can dine either in the villa at the end of the tombs, in the *triclinium* of the tombs, or on that of Actaeon, in the centre of the town, or in the *Forum*, which last will be sunny and warm, just as you please. If you accede to these propositions let me know what dish or dishes I shall bring in my pocket for the public good." On another occasion Gell begins a letter to Lady Blessington asking her to postpone a visit, because "the devil had upset his inkstand in the clouds". He said he could "teach her Italian in two hours, and, as you are a professor of Pausanias already, would willingly have a set-to at a little bit of it with you". Lady Blessington remarks that Gell "can be irresistably comic and makes one laugh for hours at his drollery".

Lady Blessington gives many amusing pen portraits of their circle at Naples, among them being the diplomatists, Sir William Drummond, Mr. William Hamilton and Viscount Ponsonby – She writes, "it is very amusing to observe the difference that exists between the minds of Sir William Drummond and Sir William Gell. That of the first, elevated and refined to such a degree, that a fastidiousness of taste, amounting almost to a morbid feeling of uneasiness in a contact with inferior intellects is the result; a result which not all his good-breeeding can prevent from being perceptible to those who are quick-sighted. That of the other, not elevated by its great acquirements, but rendering them subservient to the bent of his humour, converts them into subjects of raillery and ridicule, very often piquant, and always droll." Then there is the venerable and much-loved Archbishop of Taranto; artists and sculptors such as Thomas Uwins and Sir Richard Westmacott; The astronomers, Giuseppe Piazzi and Sir John Herschell; the geologist, Abbé Monticelli; the distinguished *littérateur*, Giuseppe Salvaggi, and the poet, Casimir de la Vigne – Antiquaries are represented by Mr. James Millingen and Mr. Thomas Matthias. Writing in 1833 of the latter, Sir William Gell says, "aged 81, is rather younger than ever, but complains that he sees nobody. Craven had him to dinner, and remarked how clever he was at contriving to ask questions without ceasing, yet never to profit in the least by the answer." There is also the Bosom friend of Gell, the Hon. Keppel Craven, son of the "beautiful Lady Craven", later Margravine of Anspach, and other visitors to Naples such as Lord Guildford, the eccentric Lord Dudley, Mr. George Howard, later Lord Morpeth and Earl of Carlisle, and Henry Fox, later Lord Holland.

Lady Blessington was an indefatigable sightseer and gives us most interesting and often amusing accounts of her excursions. Among many places she visited were Herculaneum, Pompeii where a gourmet feast was provided by Gell, Paestum where they partook of another "collation that would have shamed the Sybarite inhabitants", and Benevento where she "did not disdain the discomforts of the animated inhabitants" of the inn. There were visits to Capri and Ischia in the yacht *Bolivar* which Lord Blessington had purchased from Lord Byron. An account of the ascent of Vesuvius on asses is related with merriment and disregard of discomforts. She happens to be at La Favorita, the King's residence at Portici, when Ferdinand arrives and she gives us a rather endearing portrait of the old King. Lady Blessington is still at Naples when he dies and she goes to his lying-in-State. The Empress Marie-Louise comes to Naples and "a less interesting woman I seldom beheld" was Lady Blessington's first impression. We are told of the occasion when the bed of the King's granddaughter, Princess Christine, was struck by lightning when she was lying in it.

Relating a visit to the San Carlo Opera House, she remarks that "where the English talk music, the Italians feel it", and much detailed discussion is given with obvious learning and insight to the exhibits in the Museo Borbonico. On comparing the Greeks and the Romans, she says, "had fat beef and porter been the prevalent food and beverage of Greece, we should not behold the works that now delight us".

Local customs, the dress of the inhabitants and Neapolitan food are all commented upon – As regards the Neapolitans themselves she suggests that "the burning lava of their craters had a magnetic influence over their temperaments".

The death of Lord Byron ("that wayward and spoilt child of genius") occurs while the Blessingtons are at Naples. Lady Blessington reflects on this with much sadness and composes two poems, here given in *Appendix B*. The earlier part of *The Idler in Italy*, which is not published in this edition, prints that part of the journals relating to the Blessington's visit to Genoa in the Spring of 1823 and their encounter with Byron. Later Lady Blessington was to publish her well-known *Conversations of Lord Byron with the Countess of Blessington*.

The more I reflect on Lady Blessington's journals, the more I am impressed by her profundity of thought, the perspicacity of her judgements and her interest in the fundamental values of life.

As regards the illustrations in this book, I have been unable to trace any other portraits of Lady Blessington except that by Lawrence and the engraving by H. T. Ryall, which was taken from a portrait by A. E. Chalon and exhibited at the Royal Academy in 1834. This portrait was one of the few things she refused to part with when her possessions were sold in 1849. To my knowledge, the last record of it was when it was sold at Christie's on 18 May 1903 among other items from the estate of Sir Robert Rawlinson when it was bought by Messrs. Leggatt Bros. Since their files were destroyed in the last war, there remains no record of the subsequent purchases.

Madden (vol. i, pp. 174–6) says that in May 1849, when her possessions were sold at Gore House after her departure for Paris, many pictures were sold including "portraits by Lawrence, sketches by Landseer and Maclise and innumerable other artists". The Lawrence portrait, which cost £80, was sold for £336 to the Marquis of Hertford and remains in the Wallace Collection. Campbell Lennie in his recent biography of Landseer refers to Landseer's drawing of Lady Blessington and portrait of her hound (given to her by King Ferdinand) entitled, "Waiting for the Countess". Madden reports that the sale of the "celebrated picture of her spaniel" by Landseer brought £150 10s. at the sale.

It is of interest to note what Captain Gronow[1] tells us of Lady Blessington's appearance later, of course, than the time she was at Naples. "Those who like myself, are old enough to recollect the beautiful Lady Blessington in her brightest days, can remember that she always wore a peculiar costume, chosen with artistic taste to suit exactly her style of beauty. The cap she was in the habit of wearing has been drawn in Chalon's portrait of her,

---

[1] *Reminiscences and Recollections of Captain Gronow (1810–60)*, abridged by John Raymond, London, 1964, pp. 240–1.

well-known from the 'Keepsake', and in the shop windows of the day. It was a 'mob-cap' behind, drawn in a straight line over the forehead, where, after a slight fulness on each temple, giving it a little appearance of wings, it was drawn down close over the cheeks, and fastened under the chin. Nothing could have been more cunningly devised, or to conceal the too great width of the cheeks, and a premature developement of double chin. Lady Blessington had also a style of dress suitable to her figure, which was full, but then not 'of o'er grown bulk'. She always wore white in the morning, a thick muslin dress, embroidered in front and lined with some bright colour, and a large silk bonnet and cloak to match. This was her costume in London, but, on her arrival in Paris, two or three French ladies got hold of her, declared she was *horriblement fagotée*, and insisted on having her dressed in quite a different style by a fashionable *modiste*; they managed so completely to transform her that in the opinion of myself and all who had seen her in England, her defects were brought out, and all her beauty disappeared."

The drawings by Antonio Senape are taken from an album in my possession which bears a bookplate with the coat of arms of Rycroft. The drawing of the Port of Naples showing the *Immacolatella Vecchia* seems to be by another hand.

The most comprehensive work on Lady Blessington is R. R. Madden's *The Literary Life and Correspondence of the Countess of Blessington*, New York, Harper and Brothers, 1866. 2 vols., and Michael Sadleir's *Blessington-d'Orsay. A Masquerade*, London, Constable, 1933 is a brilliant and inspired exposition of that strange friendship. I am indebted to both these works for much of what I have written in my account of Lady Blessington's life. Both these books give lists of the writings of Lady Blessington herself as well as of other relevant publications. Bibliographies printed in *The Bourbons of Naples* and *The Last Bourbons* by Harold Acton, London, Methuen, 1956 and 1961; and also in my book *Ramage in South Italy*, London, Longmans, 1965, list many publications relating to persons, places and events in the Kingdom of the Two Sicilies.

EDITH CLAY

The
Neapolitan Journals
of
Lady Blessington, 1823–1826

(Abridged)

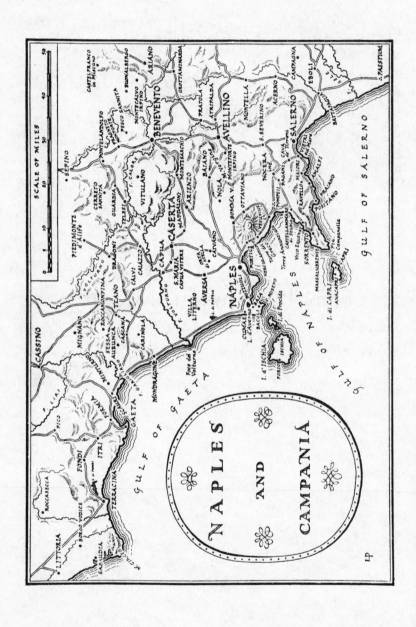

The Neapolitan Journals of Lady Blessington

July 17th, 1823.

Naples burst upon us from the steep hill above the Campo Santo, and never did aught so bright and dazzling meet my gaze. Innumerable towers, domes, and steeples, rose above palaces, intermingled with terraces and verdant foliage. The bay, with its placid waters, lay stretched before us, bounded on the left by a chain of mountains, with Vesuvius, sending up its blue incense to the Cloudless sky. Capri, behind which the sun was hiding his rosy beams, stood like a vast and brilliant gem, encircled by the radiance of the expiring luminary, which was reflected in the glassy mirror that bathed its base; and to the right, lay a crescent of blue isles and promontories, which look as if formed to serve as a limit to the waters that lave their bases. The scene was like one created by the hand of enchantment, and the suddenness with which it burst on us, added surprise to admiration. We ordered our postilions to pause on the brow of the hill, that we might gaze on the beautiful panorama before us; and as our eyes dwelt on it, we were ready to acknowledge that the old Neapolitan phrase of *Vedi Napoli e poi mori*, had a meaning, for they who die without having seen Naples, have missed one of the most enchanting views in the world.

We paused on the brow of the hill, and while the eye drank in this scene of life and beauty, one of the postilions directed our attention to a large square of ground inclosed by high walls, round which grew groups of cedars, stone-pines, and other trees, which served to break its dull uniformity: and said, "That is the Campo Santo." This melancholy spot lies to the left of the road in a defile at the bottom of the hill, divided from the route by a sort of common, on which several large and picturesque trees were scattered. There came a sudden sadness over my feelings as my eye turned from the glowing and lovely scene around, to this lonely and desolate resting-place of the dead. The contrast was effecting, and effectually sobered the rapturous admiration in which I was indulging.

18th. – I thought last night as I stood on the balcony, that the view of this lovely bay by moonlight could not be equalled; but when I looked on the same scene this morning as a brilliant sun was beaming, it seemed to have acquired greater charms. Our hotel fronts the sea, and is only divided from it by the garden of the Villa Reale,[1] which is filled with plants and flowers, mingled with statues and vases, whose whiteness is finely contrasted by their rich and vivid tints. The blue and beautiful sea is seen sparkling through the opening of the trees; and many a white sail is floating over its placid bosom. What a picture is now spread before me, and how poor, how colourless are words to paint it!

Our hotel, the Gran Bretagna, is an excellent one; the rooms spacious and well furnished, and the attendance good. Its only defect is that, being in the Strada de Chiaja, which is the fashionable evening promenade, the noise and dust are troublesome. I feel as if I should never tire of gazing on the enchanting view from my windows; and every change in the atmosphere gives a new aspect to it. How light and elastic is the air! Respiration is carried on unconsciously; and existence becomes a positive pleasure in such a climate. Who that has seen Naples can wonder that her children are idle, and luxuriously disposed? To gaze on the cloudless sky and blue Mediterranean, in an atmosphere so pure and balmy, is enough to make the veriest plodder who ever courted Plutus abandon his toil and enjoy the delicious *dolce far' niente* of the Neapolitans.

19th. – I have determined to find a suitable abode before I begin the round of sight-seeing here; for the noise of the Strada de Chiaja of an evening is so overpowering that a longer séjour in this hotel is not desirable. I devoted a considerable portion of yesterday to house-hunting; and though I have seen many fine palaces, I have not yet met with one quite to my fancy, for all are fitted up more with a view to show than comfort.

[1] The Royal Palace was built in 1600 by Fontana; was altered in 1734–8, was damaged by fire in 1837 and was finally restored by Gaetano Genovese between 1838 and 1842.

1　Lady Blessington by Sir Thomas Lawrence, 1822
(The Wallace Collection)

2 Lady Blessington by H. T. Ryall, engraving
1834 (National Portrait Gallery)

3　Prince of Belvedere by Angelica Kauffman
(Pinacoteca Nazionale di Capodimonte)

4 Salone Grande, Villa Belvedere

5 (left) Lord Blessington
by J. Holmes, *c.* 1810-20

6 (right) Count Alfred
d'Orsay by G. Hayter, 1839
(National Portrait Gallery)

7 (below) Giuseppe
Capecelatro, Archbishop of
Taranto, by Count d'Orsay,
1825

8 Naples by de Vito, *c.* 1820

9 Port of Naples, Immacolatella Vecchia

10   Miracle of St Januarius
by G. Gigante (Museo
Nazionale di Capodimonte,
Naples)

11   Villa Favorita
by F. Sicuro (Museo di San
Martino, Naples)

12 Paestum. Temple of Neptune by Antonio Senape

13 Neapolitan Mother teaching her Child the Tarantella, by T. Uwins (Victoria & Albert Museum)

14 Sorrento by Antonio Senape

The gaiety of the streets of Naples at night is unparalleled. Numberless carriages of every description are seen rolling along. The ice-shops are crowded by the *beau monde*, and the humbler portable shops, with their gaudy decorations, which are established in the streets, are surrounded by eager applicants for the *sorbetto* and lemonade, of which the lower classes consume such quantities. When I last night beheld numbers of both sexes flocking round the vendors of iced water and lemonade, I thought of the different and far less pleasing sight, which the streets of London present at the same hour; when so many persons of both sexes flock to these degrading receptacles of folly and vice, the gin-shops, to seek in the excitement of ebriety forgetfulness of cares. Here, all are gay and animated; from the occupants of the coroneted carriage down to the *lazzaroni*, who, in the enjoyment of the actual present, are reckless of the future. At one spot was seen one of those portable shops, peculiar to Naples, gaily painted and gilded, and illuminated by paper lanterns in the shape of balloons, tinted with the brightest colours, round which groups were collected devouring marcaroni, served hot to them from the furnace where it was prepared. At another shop, iced water-melons were sold in slices; the bright pink of the interior of the fruit offering a pretty contrast to the vivid green of the exterior. *Frittura*, sending forth its savoury fumes, was preparing at another stall; and *frutti di mare* was offered for sale on tables arranged along the Strada di Santa Lucia. The sounds of guitars were heard mingling with the joyous laugh of the *lazzaroni*; and the dulcet voices of the groups in carriages who accosted each other with the animation peculiar to Italians, as their vehicles encountered on the promenade. The sweet-sounding words *signorina*, *amico*, *cara*, and *carissimo*, often broke on the ear: and above this scene of life and gaiety, this motley assemblage of the beautiful and the grotesque, was spread a sky of deep azure thickly studded with stars, whose dazzling brightness seemed to shed warmth, as well as light, over the moving picture. The contrast between the solitude and silence of Rome at night, with the hilarity of the crowds that fill the streets at Naples, is striking. The people of the former partake the character of the Eternal City. They appear as if touched by the grandeur of the ruins that surround them; and are grave and dignified. The Neapolitans, like their volcanic country, are never in a state of repose. Their gaiety has in it something reckless and fierce; as if the burning lava of their craters had a magnetic influence over their temperaments.

Vesuvius sends up its blue smoke in a shadowy column, so faint as to give little indication of our being likely to witness an eruption for some time; but I never turn my eyes to it without likening it to a sleeping giant, who will wake refreshed from his slumber to make all around tremble at his power.

20th.— After having looked at half the palaces at Naples and its immediate environs, I have at length engaged the Palazzo Belvedere, at Vomero, one of the most beautiful residences I ever beheld, in the midst of gardens, and overlooking the Bay. The view it commands is unrivalled; and the gardens boast every rare and fragrant plant and flower that this delicious climate can produce. I long to take possession of it; but, alas! some days must elapse before it can be made ready for our reception, for it requires so many of the comforts indispensable to an English family, that their absence could not be compensated by the painted and gilded ceilings, oriental alabaster architraves, marble floors, pictures, and statues, with which the palace is abundantly supplied. The Prince[1] and Princess Belvedere looked surprised when I had an upholsterer to note down the different articles of furniture requisite for him to supply; as they thought the heavy, cumbrous gilt chairs and sofas, ranged in formal rows along the apartments, and the scanty furniture of the bed-rooms, amply sufficient for our wants, as they had been for theirs. House-rent is extravagantly high at Naples; and when fine suites of rooms are required, larger prices are demanded than in London.

21st. – So far from getting accustomed to the beauty of this place, it creates an increased admiration every day. The resplendent skies, and the glorious sea that mirrors them, fill me with delight: all charms, except the never-ceasing noise of the people, which overpowers and fatigues me. The drives are delightful, the sea always in view, and its breezes light as the zephyr's breath, bear freshness on their wings. We drove along the Mergellina last evening, passed through the Grotto di Posillipo, and along the Strada Nuova. What a succession of beautiful views, each acquiring new charms from the changes in the atmosphere. From a

[1] Carlo Carafa di Roccella, marchese d'Anzi and principe di Belvedere.

golden hue, in which the skies, sea, and promontories were steeped in a yellow light, like some of those pictures by Claude Lorraine, on which the eye delights to dwell, they changed to a tint of deep glowing rose; and then deepened into purple, which gave the whole scene the effect of being viewed through a coloured glass.

Emerging from the sombre Grotto di Posillipo, the dazzling picture that meets the eye is magical. This grotto is 2,316 feet in length, hewn through the solid rock, and lighted by lamps, which burn night and day. Three carriages may pass abreast without inconvenience, save from the dust which the wheels of the vehicles and horses put in motion, and which exhales a disagreeable odour. Images and pictures of saints are hung on the sides of the cavern, with small votive lamps burning before them; but the presence of these symbols of religion prevent not the loud imprecations of the coachmen, muleteers, and *lazzaroni*, which sound lugubriously amid the reverberations produced by the noise of the carriages. Entering this sombre cavern on a fine summer evening, when the sky was all splendour, its gloom and chill struck us forcibly; but when emerging from it, the enchanting prospect around seemed to have acquired greater beauty from the force of the contrast . . .

Last evening, we encountered the royal family. The King[1] was in a carriage, attended by one or two of his favourites, and the heir-presumptive to the throne, the Prince of Salerno,[2] followed in a barouche, with his wife, and the Princess Christine,[3] his daughter. The King is a thin spare man, with fresh-coloured cheeks, long nose, and grey locks, worn rather long. His countenance is animated, and he looks very hale and healthy for his years. Not so the Prince of Salerno, whose obesity indicates anything but health; and the stooping posture which he continually maintains, his head drooping over his chest, confirms the impression of helpless *embonpoint* which his countenance conveys. From this mode of holding his head, his glance has something disagreeable and sinister in it. The Princess of Salerno[4] has

---

[1] Ferdinand I, King of the Two Sicilies (1751–1825).

[2] Later Francis I, King of the Two Sicilies (1777–1830).

[3] Maria Cristina (1806–1844) who m. Ferdinand VII, King of Spain in 1829, and after his death in 1833, m. Fernando Munoz, Duke of Rianzares.

[4] Maria Isabella, Infanta of Spain, 2nd wife of Francis I, d. 1848.

been, it is said, extremely good-looking; but though only now in her thirty-eighth year, no trace of it remains: her excessive *embonpoint* having destroyed every vestige of symmetry in form and face. Her countenance is expressive of good-nature; and she returns the salutations of the crowds that pass her carriage with a good-humoured smile. The Princess Christine is in her seventeenth year, and is exceedingly pretty. Slight, and well formed, with a countenance in which *finesse* and *esprit* are delineated, even as a *grisette* she would challenge admiration. Her features are small, and neatly finished; her eyes expressive, her teeth beautiful, and her smile full of fascination. Her complexion is of a pale clear olive, which, if less brilliant than the fresh roses and lilies of the cheeks of our English ladies, is not without its charm. In short, the Princess Christine is a very attractive person, and must, without the prestige attached to the adventitious aid of royal birth, be universally considered a charming young woman. Having passed and re-passed the carriage in which she sat last evening, several times, I had good opportunities of examining her; and I must pronounce her to be worthy the admiration she excites in the combustible hearts of her countrymen; who view her less as a grand Princess, than as a very bewitching woman.

The carriages that encounter the royal cortège, draw up while they pass. The gentlemen take off their hats, and the ladies bow. Their salutations are graciously acknowledged by all the royal family, but peculiarly so by the Princess Christine, whose delicate lips expand into a sweet smile, displaying teeth like pearls, and whose bow is full of grace.

22nd. – I have been to the Palazzo Belvedere,[1] at Vomero, which now begins to wear a more habitable aspect, thanks to the activity of a French upholsterer, and some eight or ten *facchini*, who have been scrubbing it for the last two days. The only objection to Vomero, is the long and steep hill to be ascended to reach it, but it is this hill that gives it the extensive and beautiful prospect it commands, and secures to it the freshest breezes that visit the shore. A long avenue, entered by an old-fashioned archway,

[1] Now known as the Villa Belvedere. The *piano nobile* of the Villa still preserves its decoration as in the time of Lady Blessington and houses the splendid collection of pictures and works of art belonging to Maestro Ernesto Rocco. Other parts of the Villa have been converted into flats.

which forms part of the dwelling of the intendent of the Prince di
Belvedere, leads through a pleasure-ground, filled with the rarest trees, shrubs, and plants, to the *palazzo*, which forms three
sides of a square; the fourth being an arcade, that connects one
portion of the building with the other. There is a court-yard, and
fountain in the centre. A colonnade extends from each side of the
front of the palace, supporting a terrace covered with flowers.
The windows of the principal salons open on a garden, formed on
an elevated terrace, surrounded on three sides by a marble balustrade, and inclosed on the fourth by a long gallery, filled with
pictures, statues, and *alti*, and *bassi-rilievi*. On the top of this
gallery, which is of considerable length, is a terrace, at the
extreme end of which is a pavilion with open arcades, and paved
with marble. This pavilion commands a most enchanting prospect of the bay, with the coast of Sorrento on the left; Capri in the
centre, with Nisida, Procida, Ischia, and the promontory of Misenum to the right; the fore-ground filled up by gardens and
vineyards. The odours of the flowers in the grounds around
this pavilion, and the Spanish jasmine and tuberoses that cover
the walls, render it one of the most delicious retreats in the
world.

The Palazzo Belvedere contains many fine pictures, and some
good groups in sculpture. Its best picture is a Rubens, representing Herodias with the head of St. John on a charger, with Herod,
his wife, and attendants at a supper table. Four thousand pounds
have been refused for this picture. A very spirited portrait of
Masaniello, painted by his contemporary and friend, Salvator
Rosa, has attracted much notice, owing to Canova having pronounced it to bear a very striking likeness to Emperor Napoleon
when he was first consul. The walls of all the rooms are literally
covered with pictures; the architraves of the doors of the principal
rooms are of Oriental alabaster and the rarest marbles; the tables
and consoles are composed of the same costly materials; and the
furniture, though in decadence, bears the traces of its pristine
splendour. Besides five *salons de réception* on the principal floor,
the palace contains a richly decorated chapel and sacristy, a large
salle-de-billard, and several suites of bed and dressing-rooms. An
abundance of the finest and rarest porcelain vases, rock crystal,
malachite and agate ornaments, are piled on the marble tables
and consoles; and now that curtains, carpets, and other adjuncts
to comfort are beginning to be placed, the palazzo is assuming an

aspect of English elegance joined to Italian grandeur, that renders it a delightful residence.

Our banker, Mr. Price, a most gentlemanly and obliging personage, has kindly undertaken to engage Neapolitan servants for us; and, except wearing ear-rings, those he has hired look as much like London footmen as possible. I find a system of domestic economy prevails at Naples, different to that practised in all other parts of Italy, namely that an agreement is made with a cook, who furnishes all repasts required at a stipulated price per head; and each guest invited is paid for at the same rate. This system is universally adopted in all large establishments, and saves a world of trouble and imposition. A contract is entered into by which the number of *entrées, entremets, rotis, &c.* and desserts, are fixed; the *déjeuners, petits soupers, &c.* regulated, and, at the close of the week the bill, resembling that of an hotel, except that no separate items are entered, is presented and compared with the book kept as a check by the *maître-d'hôtel*. In the houses of all the *noblesse*, and even in the royal establishments, this system is pursued, and is said to give great satisfaction.

23rd. – There are many English families at Naples, – among whom Sir William and Lady Drummond[1] are conspicuous for their hospitality. Sir William Drummond is said to be unceasingly occupied in literary pursuits, and is at present engaged in his work entitled "Origines". Sir William Gell[2] is also here, and is universally esteemed and beloved; as is his inseparable friend, the Hon. K. Craven.[3] Mr. Hamilton,[4] remarkable for his erudition and taste, is our minister to the Neapolitan court; so that the residence of such men as Drummond, Gell, Craven, and Hamilton, is calculated to give the inhabitants of Naples a very high opinion of the English. Colonel Challoner Biss is also a resident at

[1] Sir William Drummond (1770–1828). Envoy Extraordinary and Minister Plenipotentiary at the Court of Naples, 1801–3 and 1806–9. He m. Harriet, d. of Charles Boone, M.P.

[2] Sir William Gell (1777–1836), the noted classical archaeologist and topographer. See *Preface*, pp. 16–18.

[3] Hon. Richard Keppel Craven (1779–1851), 3rd son of William, 6th Baron Craven and his wife, Elizaabeth, d. of 4th Earl of Berkeley.

[4] William Richard Hamilton (1777–1859). Antiquarian and diplomatist. Envoy Extraordinary and Minister Plenipotentiary at the Court of Naples, 1822–25.

Naples, where his hospitality and urbanity have rendered him very, and deservedly, popular. The Abbé[1] – fills an <u>undefined,</u> and <u>undefinable</u> position here. He is said to be in great favour with the minister, Medici,[2] and to turn that favour to a profitable account. <u>How</u> his influence with the minister has been aquired, it is not easy to imagine, for his talents are of a very mediocre kind, his manners coarse, and his reputation not honourable. *Mais n'importe*, he preserves his ground; and is received, though abused, in every great house in Naples. This is one of the many extraordinary examples one often witnesses, of a man rising from a low station without one quality to justify his ascent, or to maintain it, yet whose presence is tolerated by those who decry him.

We drove to the Mole last night, and were amused by hearing an itenerant *filosofo*, as our *laquais-de-place* called him, recite passages from Tasso's *Gerusalemme* with an earnestness, that excited no little sympathy and admiration from the circle around him. Murmurs of applause followed the pathetic parts of the poem, and showers of grains (a coin less than our farthings) rewarded the reciter. The animation with which the audience around the *filosofo* listened to passages that I should have thought too elevated for their comprehension, surprised me; and suggested the reflection of how a similar recitation would have been received by the lower classes in the streets of London. Here, the sensibilities of the people are not blunted, as with us, by the immoderate and general use of ardent spirits. The simplicity of the diet operates, I am persuaded, most advantageously, not only on the frames, but on the minds, of the Neapolitans; and leaves them free from the moody humours and feverish excitement engendered by the stimulating food and copious libations of porter and spirits to which the lower classes with us are so universally addicted.

The Mole presents the best scene at Naples for studying the tastes of the humblest portion of its inhabitants. Here they aban-

[1] (?) Abbé Campbell who, at an early age was chaplain to the Neapolitan Minister at London and who was rumoured to have married the Prince Regent and Mrs. Fitzherbert. He then left the country, and later in life took up residence at Naples where he died in 1830.

[2] Cavaliere Luigi de'Medici di Ottaiano (1759–1830), a royal counsellor and one of the highest magistrates in the Kingdom: was head of the Government and gentleman-in-waiting to the King and also Regent of the Grand Court of the *Vicaria*.

don themselves, with the gaiety of children broken loose from
school, to the impressions produced on their minds by the different persons who resort to this place to amuse them. At one spot,
the *filosofo* I named held his audience spellbound; and at no great
distance, two men sang duets, accompanying themselves on
their guitars, and making up in spirit what their music wanted in
sweetness. A *Polichine* (sic) displayed his comic powers with
irresistible humour, exciting peals of laughter from his merry
crowd; while, strange to say, a monk, mounted on a chair nearly
opposite, brandished a crucifix in the air with frantic gesture,
exhorting the followers of *Polichinel* to desert that unworthy
mime, and to follow him, who would lead them to the Re-
deemer . . .

24th. – The Honourable R. Grosvenor[1] dined with us yesterday.
He is the liveliest Englishman I have ever seen; and his gaiety sits
so gracefully on him, that it tempts one to wish it was more
frequently a characteristic of his countrymen.

I have nowhere beheld more beautiful women than in three or
four carriages at the evening drive on the Chiaja. I was peculiarly
struck by the dazzling delicacy of their complexions, a beauty
which I fancied was denied to the inhabitants of this sunny clime;
but the fairness of the ladies I have noticed, could not be surpassed in London. The Duchess di Forli,[2] one of the reigning belles of
Naples, is a lovely woman, with hair dark as the raven's wing,
and lustrous eyes of nearly as deep a hue; her complexion is of a
transparent fairness, and her lips are as crimson as the flower of
the pomegranate. The Princess Trecazi[3] is another specimen of
Neapolitan loveliness; and the Princess Centella might furnish a
faultless model for a Hebe, she is so fair, so youthful, and so
exquisitely beautiful. The expressive countenances of Italian
ladies strike those accustomed only to the less demonstrative
ones of English women, with surprise. Yet there is nothing of
boldness in their physiognomies. It is their mutable character,
changing with every emotion, and the changes conveying to the

[1] Robert, 3rd son of Robert, Earl Grosvenor, later Marquis of West-
minster (1801–1893). Created Baron Ebury in 1857.

[2] Beatrice di Sangro (1800–1859) who m. Francesco Carafa, conte di
Policastro, duca di Forlì e della Chiusa.

[3] Maria Felicia Statella, wife of Giovanni Battista Gallone, principe
di Tricase e Moliterno.

beholder the expression of the feeling of which they are the visible sign, that strike one. Their faces remind one of a beautiful lake, on whose bosom every breeze produces a gentle ripple, and every cloud its shadow; but likewise suggests the thought of what effects a storm might cause on this same beautiful surface, the mobility of their countenance indicating a more than ordinary predisposition to passionate emotions.

25th. – Palazzo Belvedere. We have taken possession of our beautiful abode, which now presents a most delightful aspect. O the comfort of finding oneself in a private house, after sojourning for eleven months in hotels! Of being sure of meeting no strangers on the stairs; no intruders in the ante-rooms; of hearing no slamming of doors; no knocking about of trunks and imperials; no cracking of whips of postilions; no vociferations of couriers; and, above all of not having our olfactory organs disgusted by the abominable odour of cigars. Surely an exemption from such annoyances, after an endurance of them for nearly a year, is in itself a subject for satisfaction; but to have secured such an abode as this *palazzo*, is indeed a cause for thankfulness. The Prince and Princess of Belvedere came to visit us to-day, and seemed perfectly astonished at the metamorphosis that we have effected in their mansion. They came to offer us the use of their box at the Opera, and many other civilities; are well bred, and appear very amiable people. The Prince was a Cardinal, but having inherited the title and fortune of Belvedere, the Pope gave him a dispensation from his vows, and the *ci-devant* Cardinal has long been a husband and father of a family.

Now that we are established in our new residence, we intend commencing a round of sight-seeing; and Naples and its environs offer occupation for many a day. So enchanting are the views from the windows of this palace, that the eye dwells on them with untiring pleasure; and when it reverts to the interior of the apartments, it is scarcely less gratified, their loftiness, spaciousness, and decorations, forming a beautiful *coup-d'oeil.*

26th. – Spent the greater part of the day at the Museo Borbonico,[1]

[1] This Museum was built in 1585 as a cavalry barracks. Count Lemos, the Spanish Viceroy, converted it into a palace for the University (1616–1777); later it became the Royal Museum and was finally taken over by the State in 1860.

which is rich in antiquities of every description, from the finest statues down to the most minute objects of a lady's toilette; some of the latter offering irrefragable proofs that the ladies of antiquity were in the habit of calling in the aid of art to heighten or repair their charms. When we behold the collections of the works of the great masters in Italy and France, and the buildings erected for them, it is impossible to resist feeling a sense of humiliation at remembering the immeasurable inferiority of similar establishments in England, where objects are crowded together in a space too small to permit their being seen to advantage. Whether this arises from want of taste, or excess of parsimony, it is equally to be regretted; and exposes our nation to many (I wish I could say unmerited) animadversions from the foreigners who visit us.

Among the statues,[1] that which most pleased me was the Aristides; the ease, yet dignity, of the posture being so wholly free from theatrical effect, which is in general the defect of statues. The drapery, too, falls admirably; and the face is full of a grave yet mild expression, that accords well with our notions of the original. Though I dislike colossal statues in general, and female ones in particular. I could not refuse the meed of admiration to the Flora Farnese; for, notwithstanding its gigantic proportions, the sculptor has skillfully managed not to destroy the feminine character of the Goddess of Flowers. The enormous size of this statue, and the feminine character still preserved in it, brought to my mind the impression I experienced on beholding Mont Blanc, one evening, when the sun was setting, and its vast and snowy surface was tinged with its rays, until the whole mountain looked a delicate rose colour; and drew from one of our party the expression, that it appeared, in its rosy drapery, an immense mass of effeminacy.

The equestrian statues of the two Balbi dissappointed me, for the horses are stiff, formal, wooden-looking ones, and their riders are nearly as precise. The Venus (I refer to the most celebrated one in this collection, for there are several) is a mere meretricious beauty, as inferior to the Medicean Venus as a pretty *danseuse* is to a lovely English girl of seventeen, on her first presentation. One can hardly believe the sex to be the same. The

[1] The statues admired by Lady Blessington can still be seen in the Museum; many of them came from the Farnese Collection, and some of them are Roman copies of Greek originals.

Agrippina is a very fine statue; there is a calmness and repose about it that characterise the works of antiquity from those of modern times. They look as if the originals, while sitting, <u>thought</u> not of placing themselves in graceful postures, but fell into them naturally; while those of our day appear studied and affected. I have never seen so perfect a personification of physical suffering as the Gladiator[1] in this Museo; but as the physical <u>only</u> is visible, it fails to excite the interest with which all must pause before its faultless rival of the Capital . . .

There is scarcely a fashion that has disfigured the female head during the last century, that may not find a prototype in the coiffures of the female busts of antiquity in the collection of bronzes here. Curls in every fantastic shape, from the Gorgon-looking locks of some ladies, to the vine tendril ringlets of others, with masses of frizzed and plaited hair, that render the countenances they were meant to adorn, hideous. The Roman busts do not realize my preconceived notion of the countenances of that people. The features are less regular than our English ones, and the faces infinitely less handsome. Indeed, it strikes me, that the Italian faces of the present day, even of the lower classes, are far more comely than those I have seen that belong to antiquity; always of course excepting the works of Grecian art, in which the faces possess not only perfect symmetry, but a peculiar expression of refinement. Long and prominent noses, with large mouths and short chins, seem to me to be the peculiar characteristics of the Roman faces of antiquity; while those of our time, if equally unmarked by a refined or intellectual expression, are certainly more comely.

27th. – Mr. R. Grosvenor and Capt. Gordon[2] dined with us yesterday; both very agreeable. The latter reminded me of his brother, Lord Aberdeen, who is a very superior man.

The gardens of the Palazzo Belvedere join those of the Floridiana, the beautiful villa of the Principessa Partanno,[3] the wife (*à la main gauche*) of the King of Naples. These left-handed marriages of Princes are by no means uncommon, and entail no

---

[1] This statue is now exhibited without its head.

[2] One of the 4 brothers of George, 4th Earl of Aberdeen (1784–1860).

[3] Lucia Migliaccio, formerly m. to the Sicilian principe di Partanno and created duchessa di Floridia by the King on their morganatic marriage.

personal disrespect on the ladies who contract them, or any political *désagrémens* on the Princes or their offspring. Titles and suitable fortunes are conferred on the ladies and their children; they are received with distinction at court, and in society, in which last, however, they are said to mingle rarely; but do not inhabit the royal residences except as visitors. The Principessa Partanno is a Sicilian lady of high birth, who being left a widow with a large family, and no longer in her *première jeunesse*, captivated Ferdinand, soon after the death of his Queen, Caroline,[1] the sister of Marie-Antoinette, who bestowed on her his left hand, the title of Princess, and a large revenue. The Principessa is much liked at Naples, and the King is said to be exceedingly attached to her; and not less so, it is stated, that she bears with great philosophy his Majesty's not unfrequent demonstrations of admiration for any pretty *danseuse*, or *chanteuse*, that appears.

The Villa Floridiana,[2] with its extensive ground, was a birth-day gift, presented by the King to this lady. His Majesty had it privately bought; repaired, and enlarged the house, which is now fitting up with a taste worthy of oriental elegance, rendered the grounds a union of classic style and arcadian beauty; and when all was nearly completed, on his birth-day, engaged the Princess to a *déjeuner à-la-fourchette*, at the Villa, and placed in the napkin, under her plate, the deed of gift.

We have free ingress to the beautiful gardens of the Floridiana, which joins ours, and in which the trees, plants, and flowers of every country are skilfully raised. Grottos, of considerable

[1] Maria Carolina (1752–1814), d. of Maria Teresa, Empress of Austria: m. Ferdinand I in 1768. Sir John Moore, writing in his diary on 7 Jan. 1807 says, "The Queen is generally called clever; she is active, meddling and intriguing. She has assumed so much of the character of a man as to make her unaimable as a woman. The late Empress Catharine of Russia is, perhaps, her model. She has, like her, a lover, but with this difference – that Catharine rewarded the lover with titles and riches but was not governed by him. The Queen of Naples has placed hers in an employment for which he has no capacity, is influenced by him, and, as he is a Frenchman, it is more than suspected that she is betrayed by him. The truth is that she is not clever, except in conversation and intrigue. She is violent, wicked, with a most perverted understanding, led by her passions and seldom influenced by reasom."

[2] Built from designs by A. Niccolini in 1817–19 and now a museum. Formerly belonged to the duca di Martina.

extent, are perforated in the huge rocks that intersect the grounds; a bridge, of fine proportion and of cut stone, is thrown across a vast chasm to unite them. Terraces of marble well executed, representing fauns, satyrs, and nymphs, with vases, and groups of sculpture, ornament the gardens. A menagerie is, in my opinion, the only drawback to this charming place, as the roaring of lions, and screams of the other wild beasts, are little in harmony with so Arcadian a spot. Never were wild beasts more carefully attended, or more neatly kept. Their cages are made to resemble natural caverns, and are cut, in fact, in rocks; and the keepers remove every unsightly object, and preserve the dens as free from impurity, as are most children's nurseries in England. I hope the mammas and nurses will pardon the comparison.

The bath in the Casino, designed for the Principessa Partano, is quite beautiful. It is a small chamber, cased with white marble, and the bath occupies nearly the whole of it, leaving only a space sufficiently large to admit of ottomans, formed of the same material, to be ranged round the room. A flight of marble steps, at each end, descends to the bath; whose dimensions would admit not only of bathing, but of swimming. A light balustrade of gilt metal encircles the bath, and from the ceiling, which is exquisitely painted with subjects analogous, descend curtains from a circular gilt ring the size of the bath, of snowy texture, which can be secured to the balustrade at pleasure. A lump of snow-white alabaster hangs from the beak of a dove over the bath. Mirrors are inserted in the marble casing of the room, and paintings of nymphs, preparing for the bath, in it, and leaving it, are placed so as to correspond with the mirrors. Marble stands for flowers are stationed near the balustrade, so that their odours may be enjoyed by the bather. The dressing-room is equally tasteful and luxurious; and no Eastern queen ever owned two more exquisitely arranged chambers. They look as if designed for some mortal, young and beautiful as the nymphs painted in them, by a youthful lover, whose mind was imbued with the luxuriant and poetical fancies of Eastern climes; instead of the person for whom this fairy palace was created, who is a grandmother, and the lover who formed it, who is an octogenarian.

28th. – We discovered last evening, that two of our Italian servants are no mean performers on the guitar, and sing well

enough to be listened to with pleasure, by even more fastidious
critics than we are. We made this discovery while sipping iced tea
last night, in the delicious pavilion, at the end of the terrace.
When first we heard the *duo*, we imagined it to be a serenade,
offered by the gallantry of some neighbour to us strangers, – no
uncommon occurrence in Italy; but on enquiring we ascertained
that the musicians were no others than two of our domestics. The
taste, the feeling, evinced by these men in their playing and
singing, quite surprised us, and must have been acquired at the
expense of considerable and patient practice.

All that I have hitherto seen of Italian servants has given me a
very favourable impression of them. They are obliging, cheerful,
and peculiarly well bred; betraying a desire not only to meet the
wishes of their employers, but to anticipate them. Our rooms are
filled with flowers every day, since our partiality for them has
been discovered; but not without a remark made by one of the
servants, of his fear of their odour being injurious to the health.
The Italian ladies have a great dread of the effect of the perfume of
flowers on their nerves; and some have been known to faint, if
not "die, of a rose, in aromatic pain." They are not equally
susceptible of unsavoury odours; for the streets through which
they must daily pass often send forth some, that are so abominable, as to induce the frequent application of a perfumed handkerchief to my nose, while they seem unconcious of the nuisance.
The odour of the flowers in Italy is infinitely more powerful than
in England; but in no part of it have I found it so strong as in the
garden here . . .

29th. – Prince Butera[1] dined with us yesterday. He is a
Hanoverian by birth, but speaks English perfectly well. He was a
soldier of fortune, went with his regiment to Sicily, where he
captivated the Princess Butera, the heiress of a very large fortune,
who bestowed her hand, wealth, and title on him; and he is now
among the most fashionable of the Neapolitan fashionables.
Strange destiny! to become from a mere soldier of fortune the
master of immense wealth, and from an obscure name, prince of
one of the most ancient titles in Sicily.

[1] Wilding, Georg, (d. 1842), a Hanovarian mercenary who m., as her
second husband, Stefania Branciforte (1788–1852), principessa di Butera,
Radalì etc.

Drove to-day to the palace at *Capo di Monte*,[1] which contains nothing worthy of remark. It was built by Charles III,[2] father to the present King who left one wing unfinished; in which state it has ever since continued. It bears much more resemblance to a barrack than to a palace, and is as uninviting a residence as possible. Some pictures by Camuccini and Landi were shown by the *custode* with as much *fierte* as if they were *chefs-d'oeuvre*: but one piece of old Gobelin tapestry, representing Admiral Coligny undauntedly facing his assassins, is, in my estimation, worth them all. This fine piece of tapestry is placed opposite to a most wretched portrait of the Princess Partanno, who is nearly as cruelly treated by the painter, as was the gallant Coligny[3] by his murderers. Never did I behold so execrable a daub. One picture in this palace I must not omit noticing. It is the portrait of the mother of the present King,[4] on horseback, dressed in the fashion of her day. A smart cocked-hat decorates her head, and her hair, which is confined behind by a ribbon, floats in the air. A pair of high boots (with spurs) covers her legs to the knees, where they are met by *une culotte*, only partly concealed by a short petticoat. A chemise with a jabot like that of a gentleman, and a cravat and waistcoat, with a pair of gauntlet gloves, complete the costume of this lady, who is mounted a *califourchon* in precisely the same attitude as the picture of the Prince Eugene.[5] A countenance of smirking self-complacency, denoting that the original of this portrait felt confident of being admired, renders the effect of the picture irresistibly ludicrous.

[1] The Royal Palace begun in 1748 by Charles III, designed by G. A. Medrano and finished between 1834–38. Now a National Museum and Picture Gallery.

[2] Charles III (1716–1788), son of Philip V of Spain and Elizabeth Farnese. Came to Italy in 1732 as heir to the Duchy of Parma and Grand Duke of Tuscany. Crowned King of the Two Sicilies in 1735, but after the death of his bro., Ferdinand IV, became King of Spain. Referred to by Sir Charles Petrie as the "perfect type of benevolent despot of the 18th century".

[3] Gaspard de Coligny (1519–1572).

[4] Maria Amalia of Saxony whose claim to distinction was the composition of hymns and lyric poetry. She died in 1738 and an anthology of her lyric poetry was published in Madrid in 1915.

[5] François Eugène, Prince of Savoy (1663–1736), youngest of 5 sons of Eugène Maurice of Savoy-Carignan, comte de Soissons – one of the greatest generals of his time.

30th. – Visited to-day the tomb of Virgil, or, at least, the spot where it is supposed his ashes repose, for on this point, as on many others, antiquarians have not quite made up their minds ...

All that remains of the tomb are four walls roofed in the form of a dome, with three windows. The building is of brick, and the exterior is covered with verdure, which gives it the appearance of a hermitage . . .

A bay-tree once crowned the tomb; but the English travellers, as the *custode* informed us, not only stripped it of its branches, but when they had all disappeared, cut the roots, so that no trace of it is left. This desire to possess memorials connected with celebrated persons is a weakness from which few are exempt; nevertheless, if we analysed the feeling, we should be led to allow that it is puerile to attach value to mere perishable memorials of even a more perishable substance, the human frame; when we have the emanations of the mind which lent the frame its honour, preserved fresh and unfading as when the immortal spark that dictated them animated its frail tenement of clay. Let us place in our libraries the works of the master spirits of past ages, instead of filling our cabinets with lumber, only prized by some remote association connected with the mortality of those whose writings are immortal . . .

Another funereal monument, near to that of virgil, excited less mournful reflections. It is that erected by an English lady to the ashes of her lap-dog! This monument has excited so much animadversion, that it is said it will be removed; and I must confess that I shall not regret its disappearance, for I do not like to see the name of her who raised it, a name honoured in Italy, as appertaining to one who has proved herself a liberal patroness of the arts, and an enlightened amateur of literature and science, exposed to the censures of those – and there are many – who think that she has insulted the ashes of Virgil, by placing those of her canine favourite so near them . . .

31st. – Went to see the Palazzo Portici[1] to-day. The situation would have been charming were it not for its close vicinity to the road, which actually passes through its court. The view from the

[1] This Palace was begun by Charles III in 1738 from designs by Medrano; was continued after 1741 by A. Canevari, and finished by F. Fuga and Vanvitelli. Was a favourite residence of Murat and is now the Facoltà di Agraria.

back of the palace, however, atones for the defect in front. It comprehends a magnificent prospect of the bay, being only divided from the sea by a garden, filled with the finest trees, plants, and flowers. No palace that I have ever seen so completely realized the notion I had formed of an Italian one, as does this at Portici. Its close proximity to the sea, whose blue waters bathe the balustrade of the garden, and the enchanting views that on each side present themselves, render it a most delicious retreat.

This residence owes all its comfort and elegance to the good taste of Madame Murat, ex-Queen of Naples,[1] who evinced not a little judgment in the alterations and repairs carried into effect in all the royal palaces during her brief reign here. The present sovereign and his family are said to have been hardly able to recognize their ancient abodes, when they returned from Sicily; and expressed no little satisfaction at the improvements that had taken place. Ferdinand is reported to have said that Murat was an excellent upholsterer, and had furnished his palaces perfectly to his taste. The apartments at Portici continue precisely in the same state as when Madame Murat occupied them; with the exception that the portraits of the imperial family have been removed to a lumber-room on the ground floor. The cipher of Murat, and the royal crown, are still attached to many of the decorations, and the lantern which lights the vestibule and grand staircase still bears them. The bed-room, bath, boudoir, and library of Madame Murat, are faultless specimens of Parisian elegance and comfort. In the *chambre à-coucher* were some drawings from the pencils of her sons, executed with great truth and spirit. They are left in the precise spots selected for them by the fond mother; and the proof of the domestic affection evinced by placing such slightly sketched drawings in so richly decorated a chamber, gave me an increased interest in the fate of her who forgot not the mother in the queen.

One of the salons at Portici[2] peculiarly attracted our attention. The ceiling and walls were covered with panels of the most beautiful china of the ancient and celebrated manufactory of Capo di Monte, of which, specimens are now become so rare. The

[1] Caroline (1782–1839), sister of Napoleon I, m. Joachim Murat, King of the Two Sicilies (1808–1815). For a description of this Palace in the time of Murat see *Italy*, by Lady Morgan, vol. iii, pp. 159–66.

[2] Was transferred to and installed in the Royal Palace at Capodimonte as were other works of art from Portici.

panels have landscapes and groups finely painted, and are bordered with wreaths of flowers the size of Nature, of the richest and most varied dyes, in *alto-rilievo*; among which, birds of the gayest plumage, squirrels and monkeys, all of china, are mingled. The chandeliers, and frames of the mirrors, are also of porcelain, and the effect is singularly beautiful. The floor was formerly covered in a similar style to the panels on the walls; but the King, when obliged to fly from Naples, intended, as it is said, to remove the decorations from this chamber, and had only detached those of the floor, when he was compelled to depart.

The portraits of the families of Napoleon and Murat are shown by the *custode*, in the small and mean apartments to which they have been consigned; and the splendour of the dresses of some of them, form a striking contrast with the rooms where they are placed; like the altered destinies of the originals, who have "fallen from their high estate." We were shown two portraits of Murat: one, a full-length, of Gérard, and the other a half-length, by a Neapolitan artist.[1] Both are considered excellent resemblances; and if so, prove that the original could not have been the handsome man he was reported to have been. An air of *braggadocio* characterises both portraits, conveying the impression of a bold captain of *banditti*, dressed in the rich spoils he had plundered, rather than of a person who had enacted so brilliant a part in the drama of life. But though the portraits have the air I have noticed, the countenance is remarkable for an expression of good humour; and I attribute the disagreeable effect produced by the pictures, to the profusion of black curls, whiskers, and moustachios, that nearly cover the face, and the swaggering posture of the figure; for the physiognomy is decidedly more expressive of good-nature than of fierceness. The children of Murat make very interesting portraits. One group is represented dancing the *tarantula*, the national Neapolitan dance; and another, the two elder sons, is painted in very rich uniforms, descending the steps of Herculaneum, attended by their preceptor and the *custode*, the light of whose torches falls on the figures of the two youths, and forms a good contrast with the darkness of the scene in which they are portrayed. A portrait of the ex-Queen of Spain, with two of her children, and pictures of some of the officers of the staff of Murat, are so execrable, that it is difficult to believe that, at such a

[1] These and other portraits of the Murat family are now in the Museo di San Martino at Naples.

recent period, the art of painting was at so low an ebb as these portraits prove it to have been; and it is still more difficult to imagine how persons accustomed to behold the treasures of art in the Louvre, could have borne to contemplate the wretched pictures at Portici. The only redeeming portrait in this collection, is that of Napoleon in his coronation robes, by Gérard, which is esteemed a fine likeness, and is well painted . . .

Murat and his wife are remembered with kindness, if not lamented, by the Neapolitans. Both were considered to possess many good qualities; and the tragical death of him to whom not even his enemies could deny the reputation of *Le brave des braves*, has made as deep an impression on his *cidevant* subjects, as their volatile natures are capable of receiving . . .

Though uneducated, the King of Naples is by no means deficient in natural ability. He is said to possess a more than ordinary degree of shrewdness; and delights in indulging in a sportive satire, always sure to be well received by his courtiers. A short time ago, when new clothing was required for the army, an officer suggested that it would be advisable to have the jacket padded over the chests, like those of the Austrians; stating that it was not only advantageous to the figure, but also served as a defence against the cut of a sabre.

"Oh, for protecting the person," replied the King, laughing, "it is much better to have the jackets padded behind."

His Majesty is passionately attached to the chase, and devotes much of his time to it. He is an excellent shot; and the salutary effects of air and exercise are very visible in his appearance, as he is one of the most healthy and active sexagenarians I ever saw.

August 2nd 1823. – Went yesterday to Pozzuoli and Baiae, and wondered not, when I beheld these enchanting shores, that they were the favourite retreats of philosophers and poets, warriors, and statesmen, who fled to them from the turmoil of busy life, to enjoy that privacy and repose which Rome denied them. The mole of the port of Pozzuoli was a noble work . . . The amphitheatre, though much impaired by the ravages of time, and by an earthquake which greatly injured it, still constitutes a fine feature in the landscape . . .

In the interior of the building is a small chapel, dedicated to St. Januarius, the patron saint of Naples, which is held in great veneration by the Neapolitans. This chapel was built to commemorate a remarkable occurrence in the life of the saint; namely, his having been exposed to be devoured by a bear of more than common ferocity; who, awed by the sanctity of the pious Bishop of Beneventum, prostrated himself before him, and became docile as a tame dove. This miracle converted not less than five thousand persons to the Catholic faith; which so enraged Timotheus, the lieutenant of the cruel Diocletian, that he had the holy man immediately decapitated. His sanguinary death led to the preservation of the blood of the saint; and to the yearly repeated miracle of its liquefaction, so edifying to the *lazzaroni* of Naples.

Our *cicerone* seemed surprised at our devoting more time to the examination of the ruins of the amphitheatre, than to the chapel of St. Januarius; and observed, that it was strange that the English invariably did so; but then added he, "they do not believe in saints, though, maybe, one day they will repent their obstinate incredulity."

The temple of Serapis next attracted our attention, and a noble ruin it is . . .

This temple was buried by an earthquake until the year 1750, when it was accidentally discovered by a peasant, which led to an excavation, that exposed these fine vestiges of antiquity to view. It is to be lamented that the Government of Naples, still more ruthless than time or the elements, has conspired to finish the work of destruction commenced by those destroyers; for columns and statues, that resisted the influence of both, have yielded to its mandates, and have been torn from the fane they adorned, to decorate palaces, or to encumber the courts of museums . . .

The vicinity of this temple is celebrated for its mineral waters, which are considered excellent in the cure of various diseases. Some modern baths have been erected on the spot, but their appliances are so disgusting, that most persons accustomed to cleanliness would prefer enduring a malady to trying the efficacy of this remedy.

In the centre of Pozzuoli stands the cathedral of St. Procule, formerly the temple of Augustus. Six Corinthian columns of great beauty, still attest the original splendour of the building . . .

We next visited the Solfatara, which offers a remarkable natural phenomenon. It bears evident marks of being the crater of an extinct volcano; and at every step, nature may be seen busy forming and crystalizing sulphur; specimens of which, in its various forms, and prismatic colours, may be viewed. On a stone being thrown against the surface of the Solfatera, it sends forth a loud reverberation, and a sound of gushing water is heard, which indicates some subterraneous river. From innumerable crevices in the white clay, liquid sulphur is seen issuing in streams; while from other fissures, vaporous exhalations are continually bursting forth. The ground shook beneath our footsteps, as we walked over the parts of the Solfatara that are passable; and on thrusting sticks into the soil, they instantly ignited, and gave a sulphurous odour.

The beautiful shore of Baiae still retains so many attractions, as to justify the preference accorded to it by the Romans; but we had not time to explore its beauties, and reserve that pleasure for another day.

4th. – The more I see of the Neapolitans, the better I like them. I have not detected among the individuals of the lower class that have fallen in my way, a single instance of the rapaciousness so generally, and I am inclined to think so unjustly, attributed to them by strangers. Their politeness has nothing in it of servility; and their good humour is neither coarse nor boisterous. The gardeners, and their wives and families, apertaining to the Palazzo Belvedere, seem actuated by an unceasing desire to please us. Fresh flowers are sent in by them, every morning, for the apartments; the finest figs, and grapes, are offered for our acceptance; and smiling faces and courteous enquiries about the health of every individual of the family meet us, whenever we encounter any of them. They sing, and not inharmoniously, while at work in the garden; occasionally *duos* and *trios*, and at other times, one begins a song descriptive of rural occupations, and his companions answer it. There is something inexpressibly charming to me, in these wild airs; but perhaps they owe much of their attraction to the delicious atmosphere in which I hear them, which disposes the mind to be pleased. No night passes in which these good people, joined by the custode and his family, do not dance the *tarantella* in the court yard, to the music of their own voices, accompanied by the *tambour de basque*. Old and young all join in this national dance, with a gaiety it is quite exhilarating to witness.

Among the various *agrémens* of the pleasure-grounds of the Palazzo Belvedere is a theatre, formed of trees and plants, the proscenium elevated, and of verdant turf, and the seats of marble; the different rows divided by cut box and ilex, which grow so luxuriously, as to screen the passages of which they form the separation. To this rural theatre it is delightful to resort, during the heat of the day; the rays of the sun being excluded by the thick foliage of the trees that surround it. Here flowers, fruit, and iced lemonade are placed, while drawing, working, and reading, occupy the individuals of our circle. From this charming retreat, it is most pleasant to see the sunbeams piercing the leafy covert that excludes their too fervid heat, and giving to the leaves of the laurels, laurustinas, and ilex, the rich tint of the emerald. The blue sky too, beheld through the openings of the foliage, looks beautiful; and, like all around, conspires to remind us that we are in a favoured clime.

We are told that the Italians writhe under the despotism of their rulers; but nowhere have I seen such happy faces. Men, women, and children, all appear to feel the influence of the delicious atmosphere in which they live; an atmosphere that seems to exclude care and sorrow. But in excluding these rude assailants of the human kind, I fear that it also excludes the grave and sober reflection so essential to the formation of an elevated mind, or to the support of a well directed one. It engenders a dreamy sort of riverie, during which, the book or the pen is often thrown down, and the *dolce far' niente* is indulged in even by those who, in their native land, have never known its effeminate pleasure. Italy is the country to which a person borne down by care, or over-worked by business, should resort. Its climate will serve as an anodyne to induce the required repose; and the happy faces that on every side present themselves, will dispose to cheerfulness. But to the ductile minds of youth, whom no care has stricken, no sorrow seared, this voluptuous region is ill suited; for vigorous must be the understanding that resists its dangerous influence. To live, is here so positive an enjoyment, that the usual motives and incentives to study and usefulness are forgotten, in the enervating and dreamy enjoyment to which the climate gives birth.

A lady talking to me, a day or two ago, on the effect of the Italian clime on female beauty, remarked that it acted as a hot-house on rose-buds, but quickly withered full-blown roses. It certainly is true, that women of twenty-five in Italy look quite as *passées*, as those of thirty-five in England; and after twenty, they lose that freshness of complexion which constitutes so great a charm in our young women. I have seen here, women quite as delicately fair, nay, perhaps, still more so, than in England; but they are deficient in that transparency of skin, through which the blood speaks so eloquently in our climate, and look rather as if blanched by the sun into fairness, than born with it. In short, they want the appearance of youth, which is the greatest charm of every face; and the absence of which no beauty can compensate.

Naples was, last night and this morning, visited by the most violent storm of thunder and lightning I ever witnessed. The flashes were so vivid, that they illuminated the rooms as if a thousand torches gleamed through them; and the thunder pealed, as if innumerable cannons were fired, the sounds loudly reverberated by the hollow soil of this volcanic country. I looked on the sea from my window, and the effect of the lightning upon it was indescribably grand. As its forked bolts, like arrows of fire, darted from the heavens, and flew along the surface of the water until they sank into its bosom, it seemed as if, at their approach, some phosphoric quality in the sea rose to meet them, in a blaze of light; while the loud thunder was heard to peal, and the earth appeared to rock to its centre. This mighty war of the elements was indeed a splendid sight, and all personal fear was quelled by its grandeur; self was forgotten in the sublimity of the scene, and one had only the consciousness of being but as an atom, too insignificant to be endangered by so tremendous an engine. There are moments when a sense of our own littleness is so forced upon us, that we think of ourselves but as motes in a sun-beam.

6th. – A visit from ——, who fills a high office at court. He told us that the lightning yesterday morning struck the bed in which the Princess Christine was reposing; and that two of her ladies who were in the apartment concluded that her Royal Highness was killed, so violent was the report of the crash, and of the falling to pieces of the bed. The Princess, without the least symptom of dismay, sprang from the fallen mattresses, before her ladies could afford her any assistance; and while they trembled at the danger to which she had been exposed, she bantered them on their pusillanimity. The courage, of which this incident furnishes an example, is said to be remarkable in one so young and delicately formed. I hope it may never be put to any worse proofs.

7th. – Sir William Gell is a great acquisition to Naples. His house is the rendezvous of all the distinguished travellers who visit it, where maps, books, and his invaluable advice, are at the service of all who come recommended to his notice. The extent and versatility of his information are truly surprising; and his memory is so tenacious, that the knowledge of any subject once acquired is never forgotten. Although a prey to disease, gout and rheumatism having deprived him of the power of locomotion, his cheerfulness is unvarying, and his temper unalterable. He opposes an unconquerable stoicism to the assaults of pain; but it is only against pain that the existence of this stern quality is made known, for a kinder heart, or one more ready to sympathize, with the cares of others, does not exist. His society is justly appreciated at Naples, and universally sought. It is curious to see him supported into a room by two persons, his body offering the melancholy picture of cureless decrepitude, while his face still preserves a youthful and healthy appearance. He is the most lively and amusing companion imaginable; possessing a perfect knowledge of life, without having lost the least portion of the freshness of mind or goodness of heart which such a knowledge is supposed to impair. He has offered to be my *cicerone* to Pompeii, and was pleased at discovering that I had studied his admirable work on it.[1]

8th. – Drove to the *Grotto dei Cani* to-day, and witnessed the cruel and daily-repeated experiment of exposing a poor dog to its mephitic vapours. The wretched animal, when called by his rapacious owner, shrank back with evident trepidation; and when seized by him whined in so piteous a manner, as to convince me how much he dreaded the trial to which he was forced to submit. He was held down close to the spot whence the noxious vapour arises, and in a very short time gave proofs of its destructive effects. His body became convulsed, his eyes glared, and his tongue protruded, and this state of suffering was followed by a total prostration of strength, and semblance of death. He was plunged into the lake Agnano, which is near the grotto; and in the space of ten minutes recovered, and assumed his

---

[1] *Pompeiana. The Topography, Edifices and Ornaments of Pompeii*, by Sir William Gell and John P. Gandy. 2 vols. There were 3 editions: between 1817 and 1819, in 1824 and in 1832.

ordinary appearance. I remonstrated with his owner on the cruelty of the treatment of this poor animal: but was answered, that "he was so accustomed to it that he did not mind it in the least, and that his apparent reluctance and whining were only proofs of his cunning," used to extort some dainty morsel from his master.

The Lago d'Agnano is also the crater of a volcano. On its banks are some ruins, said to be the remains of a villa of Lucullus, that celebrated epicurean of antiquity, whose luxurious suppers are recorded. He opened a communication between this lake and the sea, that the former might serve as a fish-pond to administer to his predominant passion for dainties. Strange and grovelling propensity, which converts the temple of the soul into the sepulchre of fish, flesh and fowl, giving to the bloated gourmand who consumes them many of the infirmities to which all gourmands are a prey.

9th. – Mr. Mathias,[1] the reputed author of "Pursuits of Literature", dined with us yesterday. He is far advanced in years, of diminutive stature, but remarkably lively and vivacious. He is devoted to Italian poetry, and is a proficient in that language, into which he has translated several English poems. His choice in the selection has not always been fortunate. He resents with warmth the imputation of having written the "Pursuits of Literature": not that he would not be vain of the erudition displayed in that work, but because some of the persons severely treated in it were so indignant, that he positively denied the authorship, though the denial has convinced no one. Mathias' conversation is interesting only on Italian literature. His <u>friends,</u> (commend me to friends for always exposing the defects or *petits ridicules* of those they profess to like) had prepared me for his peculiarities; and he very soon gave proofs of the correctness of their reports. One of these peculiarities is an extraordinary tenacity of memory respecting the dates at which he, for the first time of the season, had eaten green peas, or any other early culinary delicacy; another is the continual exclamation of "God bless my soul!" Dinner was not half over before he told us on what days he had eaten spring

[1] Thomas James Matthias (1754–1835). Satirist and Italian scholar of whom Sir William Gell remarked that he was "as obstinate as 20 pigs". Sometime Treasurer to Queen Charlotte, wife of George III, and Librarian at Buckingham House.

chickens, green peas, Aubergine, and a half hundred other dainties; and at each *entremet* that was offered him, he exclaimed, "What a delicious dish! – God bless my soul!"

Mr. Mathias has an exceeding dread of being ridden or driven over in the crowded streets of Naples; and has often been known to stop an hour before he could muster courage to cross the Chiaja. Being known and respected in the town, many coachmen pause in order to give him time to cross without being alarmed; but in vain, for he advances half way, then stops, terrified at his imaginary danger, and rushes back, exclaiming "God bless my soul!" It is only when he meets some acquaintance, who gives him the support of an arm, that he acquires sufficient resolution to pass to the other side of a street. While he was dining in a *café*, a few days ago, a violent shower of rain fell, and pattering against the Venetian blinds with great noise, Sir William Gell observed that it rained dogs and cats; at which moment a dog rushed in at one door of the *café*, and a frightened cat in at the other.

"God bless my soul," exclaimed Mathias, gravely, "so it does! so it does! Who would have believed it."

This exclamation excited no little merriment; and Mathias resented it by not speaking to the laughterers for some days.

10th. – Went to the Opera last night, but the heat was so oppressive, as to render it anything but a pleasure. The heat at Naples is different from that of Rome, and has in it a dry, scorching warmth, that reminds one that this is a volcanic country. San Carlo is a magnificent theatre, both in size and decoration. The boxes are roomy and well ventilated, and the parterre is all divided into stalls. The royal box is in the centre of the house, and forms a very striking and ornamental object. It projects considerably, is supported on gilded palm trees, and is surmounted by a large crown; from which descends, on each side, a mass of drapery, apparently of metal painted and gilt, to resemble cloth of gold, which is held up by figures of Fame. The interior is cased with panels of looking-glass; and fitted up with crimson velvet, trimmed with bullion fringe. This box is seldom occupied by its royal owner, or any of his family. His Majesty sits in a large private box, near the stage, attended by two officers of state. The hereditary Prince and Princess, with their family, which is very numerous, occupy a very large box near that of the King. The Princess Christine looked exceedingly pretty last night; and many a furtive glance was cast towards her, – a homage that did not seem offensive to her feelings, if one might judge by her countenance, although it is strongly disapproved by the elders of the royal family. Curious stories are told on this subject at Naples; and it is asserted, that more than one young noble has been advised to travel for his health, because detected in looking too often towards the pretty Christine.

Fodore and Lablache sang last night. The voice of the former has lost none of its thrilling sweetness since I heard her in London; and the latter has one of the finest voices imaginable, added to which, he is an inimitable actor. We English talk of music, but the Italians feel it. Not a sound interrupted the "Sweetness long drawn out" of the singers, who seemed aware that they were singing before competent judges, so carefully and admirably did they give the music allotted to them. None of the noisy efforts, so sure to be received with plaudits by the greater mass of an English audience, were ventured here, nor would they be tolerated. Refinement and pathos, are substituted for those loud tones we too often hear in London; which, however they may prove the force of lungs of the singer, speak little for the musical taste of his audience.

The King seems to be as partial to dancers, as to singers, for he applauded Mademoiselle le Gros last night, quite as rapturously as he had done Madame Fodore, half an hour before. I can sympathize with the love of music, in an old man, but love of dancing in a sexagenarian has something unseemly in it.

11th. – I have rarely met so gifted a person as Sir William Drummond, who dined with us yesterday. To a profound erudition in classical lore, he joins a great variety of other knowledge, being an adept in modern literature, mineralogy, chemistry, and astronomy. The treasures of his capacious mind are brought into action in his conversation, which is at once erudite, brilliant, and playful. To these qualifications for forming a delightful companion, he adds a good-breeding which, while it possesses all the *politesse* of *la vieille cour*, has nothing of its cold ceremoniousness. His mind is so thoroughly imbued with classical imagery, that his conversation might be deemed a little pedantic, were it not continually enlivened by flashes of an imagination so fertile, and a fancy so brilliant, that these natural endowments throw into shade the acquired ones, with which a life of study has enriched him. It is very amusing to observe the difference that exists between the minds of Sir William Drummond and his friend Sir William Gell. That of the first elevated and refined to such a degree, that a fastidiousness of taste, amounting almost to a morbid feeling of uneasiness in a contact with inferior intellects, is the result; a result which not all his good-breeding can prevent from being perceptible to those who are quick-sighted. That of the other, not elevated by its great acquirements, but rendering them subservient to the bent of his humor, converts them into subjects of raillery and ridicule, very often piquant, and always droll. The heroes of antiquity, when referred to by Sir William Drummond, are invested with new dignity; but when alluded to by Sir William Gell, are travestied so comically, that they become ludicrous. So far from possessing the morbid fastidiousness of his friend, with respect to his associates, Gell, though he can appreciate superior minds, can find pleasure in a contact with the most inferior, and by eliciting the ridiculous points of their characters, render them subjects of amusement. His drollery is irresistible; and what renders it more piquant is the grave expression of his countenance, which maintains its seriousness, while those around him are excited to laughter, by the comicality of his sallies. He views every object through the medium of ridicule, and as a subject for pleasantry. Even his own infirmities are thus treated by him; so that he may really lay claim to the character of a laughing philosopher, if he cannot arrogate the more elevated one of a profound thinker.

12th. – Spent several hours yesterday at the Museo Borbonico, a delightful lounge in this sultry weather.

The treasures found at Herculaneum and Pompeii possess an irresistible attraction for me, not from their singular beauty and fitness only, but from the associations they awaken. To touch objects that for many centuries were buried from the gaze of men, amid the ruins that served as a tomb to their owners, excites a feeling that no other objects of art, however beautiful, can awaken. The finest statue of antiquity gives but a personification of the *beau ideal* of the sculptor who formed it. Many living models were referred to, ere one of these *chefs-d'oeuvre* of art grew into the old but faultless beauty we gaze on. Hence, reality is lost in their perfection; while, in the busts and statues of persons discovered at Herculaneum and Pompeii, the ideal is sacrificed to truth; and an individuality is so strikingly visible in them, that one could, at a glance, pronounce that they must resemble the originals.

The busts of a young lady of the Balbi family, found at Herculaneum, and the mother of Balbus from the same place, though far from offering specimens of female loveliness, are so full of truth and nature, that a physiognomist might pronounce on their respective dispositions; and hence they possess a charm for me, not often found in more beautiful works of art.

There is no end to the pagan gods and goddesses in this museum. Minervas, Junos, and Venuses, are jostled by satyrs and fauns; and Jupiters, Apollos, Mercuries, and Cupids, are mingled among the less dignified river gods, Ganymedes, gladiators, and the more vile emperors; some of the countenances of latter bearing the impress of the vices attributed to them . . .

The works of the Greek sculptors soon make themselves felt; and even an amateur can quickly distinguish them from those of their Roman imitators. The climate of Greece must surely have had a powerful influence, not only on the persons of its inhabitants, but over the minds of its artists; or they never could have produced the *chefs-d'oeuvre* they have bequeathed to us. The diet, too, must have had its operation; and I am inclined to think that, had fat beef and porter been the prevalent food and beverage of Greece, we should not behold the works that now delight us. Neither the models nor the sculptors would have been so spiritualized; for the minds of the latter would have become as heavy as the figures of the former . . .

There is no straining after theatrical effect, in the statues of antiquity; and the absence of this meretricious and frequent fault of modern sculptors, forms one of their greatest charms. The history of the mother of Nero is impressed on this image of her; and the effect produced on the mind by its contemplation, partakes of the melancholy character that appertains to it. In a statue of Nero, in his boyhood, one looks in vain for any indication of the passions that, in maturity, rendered him a blot in human nature. The face is peculiarly handsome, and the character of the countenance is that of mildness. Yet even when this image of him was sculptured, the germs of the vices, which afterwards rendered him so fearful a monster, were in embryo; and the recollection of them impels the gazer to turn with horror from a face that otherwise might claim admiration; so faultless are its features, and so gentle is its expression. The Antinous of Naples is far inferior to that of Rome, offering merely physical beauty; while the other possesses a more elevated character.

13th. – Drove yesterday to Cumae. A delicious day; the sea blue, and calm as the skies that canopied it. Saw the vestiges of the celebrated Villa of Cicero, consisting of a subterraneous place, said by some to have been a wine-cellar, and by others, to have been a bath. The Arco Felice, which we ascended with difficulty, commands a charming prospect of the different islands with which the lovely bay is studded; and which arise from the blue waters, as if fresh from the Creator's hands; their verdure scarcely less brilliant than the liquid mirror that reflects them. Fragments of ruins, overgrown by vegetation, intersect the route at every side. Some of them are exceedingly curious and picturesque, and add greatly to the beauty of the scenery; although this union of the ruins of antiquity, with a nature so vigorous and smiling as that which surrounds them, chastens the gaiety to which so luxuriant a landscape would otherwise give birth . . .

The mind is divided between classical associations of the past, and admiration for the beauty of the present scenery, while wandering through spots described by Pliny, and sung by Virgil; whose fictions seem invested with something of truth, when we behold the sites of the scenes which he represents . . .

The Grot of the Sibyl at Cumae, is situated under the hill on which once stood the temple of Apollo, described by Virgil in the Æneid as having been built by Daedalus, to commemorate the spot where he alighted.

> 'To the Cumean coast at length he came,
> And, here alighting, built his costly frame
> Inscribed to Phoebus; here he hung on high
> The steerage of his wings that cut the sky.'

It is asserted that a subterraneous passage, close to the lake Avernus, communicated with this grotto; but the earth has fallen in, and so filled the cavern, as to preclude its being explored more than eighty or a hundred yards; nor does it, to that extent, offer any thing to repay the trouble of the explorer.

Near Cumae, are the Elysian Fields, which are approached by a path through a very pretty vineyard. The *Mare Mortuum* is passed on this route, as are several interesting ruins of sepulchres, half

covered with foliage, which have a beautiful effect. The solitude
and repose that pervade Cumae, where nought is heard but the
distant murmur of the sea, and the lively carols of the birds; and
where nought is seen but the bright verdure of this fruitful soil,
and the classical ruins that are mingled with it, have so soothing
an effect on the mind, that one wishes the importunate *cicerone*,
with his impertinent explanations, far away; that the liberty of a
solitary ramble, unbroken by his clamorous descriptions, might
be enjoyed . . .

On pausing to view the lucrine lake, our *cicerone* lamented that
it is at present innoxious, its poisonous vapours having disappeared. Birds, he remarked with a deep sigh, no longer dropped
dead when hovering near it, consequently the spot was not
nearly so much frequented, as when the lake offered this interesting sight; people always, as he said, flocking to see that which is
disagreeable, in preference to that which is beautiful . . .

It is now many days since my journal has been opened; for
idleness, the besetting sin of this place, has taken possession of
me. I shall journalize no more; but merely write down, whenever
in the humour, what occurs, or what I see. O the *dolce far niente* of
an Italian life! who can resist its influence? – not I, at least.

The streets of Naples present daily the appearance of a fête.
The animation and gay dresses of the lower classes of the people,
and the crowds who flock about, convey this impression.
Nowhere does the stream of life seem to flow so rapidly as here;
not like the dense and turbid flood that rushes along Fleet Street
and the Strand in London; but a current that sparkles while
hurrying on. The lower classes of Naples observe no medium
between the slumber of exhaustion and the fever of excitement;
and, to my thinking, expend more of vitality in one day than the
same class in our colder regions do in three. They are never calm
or quiet. Their conversation, no matter on what topic, is carried
on with an animation and gesticulation unknown to us. Their
friendly salutations might, by a stranger, be mistaken for the
commencement of a quarrel, so vehement and loud are their
exclamations; and their disagreements are conducted with a fiery
wrath which reminds one that they belong to a land in whose
volcanic nature they strongly participate. Quickly excited to
anger, they are as quickly propitiated; and are not prone to
indulge rancorous feelings . . .

The Neapolitans are even more partial to theatrical exhibitions than are the French. Numerous small theatres, the price of admission to which is so trifling that the poorest persons can command it, are crowded to excess; and the streets, squares, and mole, have itinerant performers, in the shape of rope-dancers, puppet-shows, and reciters, always surrounded by applauding audiences. Instead of printed play-bills to announce the performances in the minor theatres, the walls in their vicinity are covered with gaudy sketches of the principal scenes, which attract those who intend to witness the entertainment, and satisfy those who are too prudent to pay the admission. The King joins in the popular admiration for theatrical representations, and is not very fastidious in his taste.

Went yesterday to see the *palazzo* called the Favorita,[1] the position of which is very agreeable. While in one of the rooms commanding a view of the entrance, the King arrived in an unpretending and simple *calèche*, drawn by a pair of horses, and attended by two servants in plain liveries. He wore a grey frock coat, high boots, and a broad leafed hat. He looked the very picture of a respectable farmer: his tall and muscular figure touched, but not bent by age; his clear and ruddy complexion offering a pleasing contrast to the snowy locks and whiskers that edged his cheeks. His Majesty had scarcely entered the garden, when two of the under-gardeners ran up to him with demonstrations of the liveliest joy, and seizing the royal hands, kissed them repeatedly with a hearty warmth. The good-natured monarch permitted the familiarity with an air of benevolence very gratifying to witness, and smiled complacently at the vehement benedictions of his humble admirers, as with light but firm step, he walked rapidly from flower-bed to flower-bed, examining all.

The Neapolitan King has evidently a distaste for show and parade; and enjoys the freedom from ceremony and constraint which his simple habits have insured him. He seldom remains more than a few days at any of the royal palaces; and goes from Naples to Capo di Monte, thence to Caserta, to Portici, and the Favorita (about a mile distant) in turn, taking with him but two or three domestics. His sleeping-rooms in each of his palaces exactly resemble each other. A small, but well-ventilated apartment, a

[1] This splendid Villa with park and garden is about a mile from Portici at Resina. It was a favourite residence of Ferdinand I and Maria Carolina. Was restored in the early part of the nineteenth century by dal Fuga.

diminutive bed, with dimity curtains white as snow, and furniture of the plainest materials, but all scrupulously clean, is appropriated to the King. A dressing-closet, with every appliance for ablution, joins the sleeping-room; and the *toilette* apparatus is as unostentatious as that of any private gentleman in his Majesty's dominions. The extreme simplicity of the King's private apartments form a remarkable contrast with those of the Princess Partanno, which combine all that luxury can suggest, or wealth supply. The Favorita contains nothing worthy of note.

Went to see the Archbishop of Tarentum[1] yesterday. Fame has not exaggerated the attractions of his manner, or the charms of his countenance, in both of which the most winning suavity and benevolence are visible. The refined politeness that characterizes his manners is mingled with a warmth that renders them very fascinating. It was pleasant to see the effectionate terms on which he and Sir William Gell are; and to observe the interest he takes in every new discovery in art and science. This amiable and venerable prelate, so universally beloved by his compatriots, and so much esteemed and respected by ours, is now far advanced in years; but his mental faculties are in full vigour. His conversation is lively and animated, abounding in information, which is never obtruded to display the extent of his erudition, but is introduced according to whatever subject others converse on. He possesses some very fine pictures, and rare antiquities, which he takes great delight in showing: among the latter, are two *bassi-rilievi* of mosaic, considered to be most rare, if not unique.

The Archbishop presents the most perfect personification of the *beau-idéal* of a venerable father of the church, that I have ever beheld. His face, peculiarly handsome, is sicklied o'er with pale hue of thought; his eyes are of the darkest brown, but soft, and full of sensibility, like those of a woman. His hair is white as snow, and contrasts well with the small black silk *calotte* that crowns the top of his head. His figure is attenuated, and bowed by age, and his limbs are small and delicate. His dress is neat even to elegance, and his whole appearance must strike every beholder as being one of the most prepossessing imaginable. He has

[1] Giuseppe Capecelatro (1744–1836). Sir William Gell relates that when visiting the Archbishop he often found him at table with his two cats sitting on stools on either side of him and the Archbishop feeding them from his plate.

given us a pressing invitation to come often to visit him; a privilege of which I intend to avail myself.

Pompeii[1] has surpassed my expectations. I could not have seen it under more favourable auspices; for Sir William Gell, who has studied it *con amore*, accompanied us. Every step taken in this City of the Dead, teems with recollections of the past, and offers subjects for meditation. We entered Pompeii by the Street of the Tombs, which presents one of the most striking and impressive scenes imaginable. On each side, elevated above the footway, a succession of funeral monuments meets the eye, many of them in fine preservation, beautiful in design and execution, and with their inscriptions still undefaced, – the destruction that over-whelmed the habitations of the living, having been more lenient to the homes of the dead. The Romans had a fine moral intention in placing the tombs of the dead in public situations; for not only were reflections on the brevity of life thus brought more fre-quently and impressively before them, but an incitement was given to merit posthumous distinction, by having the honours rendered to the great and good of the departed continually dis-played before the eyes of their survivors.

The streets of Pompeii are paved with blocks or lava, well joined together, and the marks of wheels are visible in many of them; but the chariots, and their drivers – where are they? This use of lava proved the occurrence of an eruption previous to the one so destructive to this city; although there is, I believe, no record to be found, of any prior one, in history. At each side of the streets are raised *trottoirs*, divided from the centre by kerb-stones, pierced for chains to pass through them. On approaching the Herculaneum gate, by which Pompeii is entered from the Naples road, a large pedestal is observed on the left, supposed to have borne a colossal statue of bronze, some fragments of a drapery of that metal having been found close to it. On the right is an arched alcove, round which is a bench of marble. An altar, with a very beautiful bronze tripos, stood in the centre, (now in the museum), and this gave rise to the supposition that the alcove was dedicated to some sylvan deity. To me it appeared simply as a *reposoir*, erected for the convenience of persons to wait until the gate was opened, as it stands very close to it. The gate, although

[1] For a general account of this site see Raleigh Trevelyan: *The Shadow of Vesuvius. Pompeii A.D. 79*, London, Michael Joseph, 1976.

the principal entrance to Pompeii, is not remarkable for its design or execution. It consists of an archway in the centre for carriages, with an opening at each side for pedestrians, and is built of brick and faced with *stucco*, on which many inscriptions and ordinances are visible. A skeleton, with a spear still grasped in its hand, was found in the *reposoir*, and is supposed to have been that of a sentinel, who met death at his post, the spear held even in death attesting his constancy to duty. This gate is by no means in harmony with the Street of Tombs, to which it forms the entrance; and the pure white of the marble of which the monuments are composed is strangely contrasted with the discoloured cement that covers it. The villa named Suburbana, but better known as that of Diomedes, next attracts attention. It is considered to be one of the most spacious, but in its general construction bears little indication of good taste. It is placed on an eminence, gently sloping towards the sea, and consisted of two stories. The best rooms opened on a terrace, extending the length of the house, and above a garden. The basement story has an arcade in front, and comprises several apartments, which, like those above them, have painted walls and mosaic pavements. One of these rooms had a large glazed bay window, of the glass of which particles were found, set in leaden frames. A bath, with every possible appendage for comfort, was among the *agrémens* of this villa; and proves that its owner understood the advantage of this healthful and luxurious mode of ablution, so much more generally in use with foreigners than with us.

Sir William Gell called our attention to the *cavoedium* in this villa, as being the largest at Pompeii. The centre of the roof is supported by peri-styles, and water is conveyed by a channel into cisterns at the extremities of the *cavoedium*, with *puteals* placed over them. The columns are covered with stucco, and painted red, which has a very bad effect. The portico around the garden is extremely poor, the piers thin, and the openings alternately wide and narrow. In the cellars are several earthen *amphorae* ranged against the walls, in the same order in which they stood two thousand years ago. They are filled with an earthy substance, portions of which have cemented the amphorae together, as if glued to each other. Twenty-three human skeletons were found in these cellars, supposed to have been the remains of those who had fled thither for refuge in the first hours of destruction, but who only found there a prolongation of their sufferings; for the

volcanic matter penetrated through the loop-holes of the building in so impalpable a powder, that it must have taken some days
to have filled the cellars sufficiently to have caused suffocation,
by which it is imagined those wretched mortals met death. The
impressions of the forms of some of the persons are still visible on
the walls against which they reclined, the moist powder having
formed moulds round them.

Various ornaments, chiefly female ones, were found with the
skeletons, as also coins of gold, silver, and brass. At the entrance
of the house two skeletons were discovered; one still grasped a
purse containing many coins and medals, – proving that avarice,
the ruling passion, was strong even in death, – while the other
hand held the key of the dwelling. Vases of bronze, and other
articles of value, were found near the other skeleton.

This villa, when first discovered, was supposed to have been
that of Cicero, referred to in his letters to Atticus; latterly, however, it is affirmed to have belonged to Diomedes, a magistrate of
Pompeii; but both suppositions are supported by conjecture
only. Sir William Gell pointed out to us some ruined buildings in
Pompeii, the appearance of which indicate that their destruction
was prior to the general one that overwhelmed the city; and this
he receives as proof of the statement of Seneca, that Pompeii
suffered severely by an earthquake in the ninth year of the reign
of Nero, sixteen years previous to the eruption. The inhabitants,
although they had commenced, had not completed the restoration of many of the buildings, which accounts for the unfinished
state in which many of them have been found. The repairs speak
little for the taste of the Pompeians, as, in most instances, that
which appears to have been originally good, has been spoilt in
the restoration. For example, in the Temple of Venus, several
Grecian entablatures, in tolerable taste, have been barbarously
plastered over and painted, transforming them from a pure Grecian to a bad Roman style. In many buildings we observed Ionic
columns formed of *tufo*, cased by brickwork, plastered over, and
painted to resemble doric. Nothing can be more meretricious
than the general effect of these painted columns; indeed, in all
parts of Pompeii, purity of taste has been sacrificed to glare and
gaudiness of decoration. So ill-constructed, too, were the
houses, that they owe their durability solely to the cement, so
lavishly used that every wall was encased in it, and in many
instances, the *stucco* was not less than six inches thick.

The Temple of Jupiter, supposed by some to have been that of Ceres, is a parallelogram. The columns are in *tufo*, thickly encased with cement, and are of the Corinthian order: the capitals are said to resemble those of the circular Temple of Tivoli. The ceiling of the portico, being of considerable width, must have looked heavy, from the want of internal columns to support it; the side columns are too close to the wall, leaving the space too wide for the length, and for the effect of the ceiling. The side walls are painted in panels, with a variety of ornaments, which look paltry, and unsuitable to the interior of so large a temple; and the unity of the design is much impaired by a small building at the end, added, most probably, subsequently to the completion of the temple.

The houses in Pompeii are, for the most part, on a small scale. They have a court of narrow dimensions in the centre, around which the apartments branch off, and into which they open. The rooms are lighted only by apertures in, or above the doors, or sometimes by a scanty window into the court; and are so small and ill-ventilated, as to confirm the received opinion, that the Pompeians spent but little of their time in their dwellings, save for the purposes of eating or sleeping. Consequently, it may be supposed that they were unacquainted with the elegancies and comforts of <u>home</u> – that blessing, the very name of which calls up so many fond and delightful associations to our minds. The number and extent of the theatres of the ancients prove that the privacy of domestic life was little known amongst them; and that the hours not occupied by business were devoted to public amusements. Some few of the houses were, however, on a larger scale, and retain traces of elegance in their interior arrangements. The dwellings of Pansa, and of Sallust may be ranked among the most superior of these. The *cavoedia* in both are larger and better lighted, having a dome or *impluvium*, which conveyed water into a marble basin in the centre of the apartment, which basin was called a *compluvium*, and gave coolness to the air, in a climate, and in apartments where it must have been so much needed. Beyond the *cavoedium* was the peristyle, into which opened the eating-room, with its *triclinium*. The apartments of the women were serarated from those of the men by the peristyle, into which they opened. The walls of these various rooms still retain fragments of the paintings that once ornamented them, possessing a degree of spirit and beauty that prove the excellence which the Pompeians had attained in this branch of the fine arts, the pavements, too, exhibit some good specimens of mosaic.

Glad as I was to profit by the *savoir* of Sir William Gell, whose acquaintance with Pompeii and its antiquities renders him the best *cicerone* in Italy, yet I could have wished to ramble alone through this City of the Dead, which appealed so forcibly to my imagination, conjuring up its departed inhabitants, instead of listening to erudite details of their dwellings, and the uses of each article appertaining to them . . .

On finding myself occasionally alone in some apartment of the dwellings in Pompeii, the paintings still fresh and glowing on the walls, and the pavements with their bright devices still unfaded, I felt as if intruding, an unbidden guest, in some mansion, whose owners had but lately left it: and the echoes of the voices of my companions, from other buildings, sounded strangely in my ears, as if they were those of the departed hosts, reproaching me for thus unceremoniously exploring the secret recesses of their domestic privacy . . .

My eyes involuntarily turned to Vesuvius, the cause of the destruction around me. There it was, tranquil as a sleeping child, and bearing no indication of its dangerous properties, save a light blue smoke, ascending to the sky, like that seen floating from some peaceful cottage in happy England . . . It seemed all a dream; and the fearful past appeared more real to the imagination than the calm and smiling present: the ruins around alone attesting that Destruction had been here.

The view from the gallery of the amphitheatre is beautiful. The Bay of Naples seen stretching out on one side, and the coast of Castellammare on the other, with the inland country in the background. The interior of this fine theatre was decorated with paintings, of which but faint traces now remain, the exposure to the weather having nearly destroyed them. The guides have adopted a plan that must eventually efface all the paintings, and which really calls for the interference of those who have power to put a stop to it. I refer to their constant custom of throwing buckets water on the painted walls, which process gives a momentary vividness to the pictures, but must soon destroy them. I never rejoiced more in being blessed with personal agility than while exploring Pompeii, for it enabled me to descend from the ass on which I was mounted, and to escape from the erudite explanations of my grave and learned *cicerone*, to scramble over

wild banks of vineyards, and mounds of earth, in order to explore some tempting-looking court of a building, or to watch the progress of the excavations . . .
[For Lady Blessington's Poem *To Pompeii* see *Appendix B.*]

The Forum Vinalia was the spot fixed on for our halting-place; and, on arriving there, we found a *recherché* collation spread on the tables, shaded by weeping willows, the bright foliage of which formed an agreeable protection against the scorching rays of the sun. The table covered with snowy napkins, and piled with every dainty of the united *cuisine à-l'anglaise, française,* and Neapolitan; from the simple cold roasted meats and poultry, to the delicate *aspics, mayonnaises, Galantine de volaille, pains de lièvre aux pistaches, pâtes de Pithiviers, salades d'homard et d'anchois,* and *la Poutarga,* down to all the tempting *friandises à-la-napolitaine,* formed as picturesque an object to the sight, as a tempting one to the palate. Sir William Gell was eloquent in his praises of our superiority over the ancients in the noble science of gastronomy; asserted that Pompeii never before saw so delicious a *déjeuner à-la-fourchette,* and only wished that a *triclinium* was added to the luxuries, that he might recline while indulging in them: a position, however, which I should think far from agreeable when eating.

"There are no people like the English," said Sir William Gell; "they transport with them to every clime the luxurious habits, and appliances that administer to them, of their own. Here we are, with a table as elegantly served, as if in a grand mansion in London, or delightful villa at Richmond. The viands of the rarest and choicest quality, as Mr. Gunter[1] would say; every delicacy, not only of the season, but of different seasons and countries, with all appliances to boot, of silver plates, dishes, and forks, &c. &c., in the middle of Pompeii! Iced wine, too, I declare! Commend me to my grumbling compatriots, who carry with them all the creature comforts that can alleviate, if not subdue, their natural disposition to find fault. They never gratify one sense without attending to the wants of another. Sight-seeing is proverbially an occupation that incites hunger; and they, above all other people, prepare for its indulgence."

[1] James Robert or John Gunter of Negri and Gunter, well-known Caterers of Berkeley Street who specialized in Neapolitan pastries and ices.

Our party rendered ample justice to the repast, and while doing so; it was amusing to look on the faces of the attendants, and to hear the mixture of different languages. The brown-haired Englishman with ruddy complexion, the yellow-haired German, the swarthy Italian, and the animated Frenchman, presented as distinct physiognomies as the languages they spoke. The jumble amused Sir William Gell very much; and he drew from all, except the Englishmen, some amusing remarks. An English servant is the only one who is never betrayed into even the semblance of familiarity; a fact which once led an Italian noble to remark, that the cause of the appearance of hauteur so visible in the upper classes of the English, originated in the extreme distance observed towards them by their servants, instead of attributing the distance to the decorum preserved by the masters . . .

Sept. 7th 1823. – The wife of one of the gardeners of Belvedere was confined this morning, and gave birth to a fine little girl. I saw her at work in the courtyard an hour before the event, and in less than an hour after it had occurred, the infant was brought to me, swathed in the Italian mode from the chest to the feet, precisely like the drawings of Indian children which I have seen. The head had no cap, but was profusely powdered, and strange to say, the ears were already pierced, and bore gold rings in them. The powdered head formed a curious contrast with the red face of the infant, which presented any thing rather than a pleasing sight: nevertheless, the relatives and friends of the parents pronounced it to be the most charming *bambino* ever seen, and the mother pressed it rapturously to her breast, as, seated beneath the arcades in the court, within six hours after her *accouchement*, she exhibited it to her neighbours and visitors, with no small degree of self-complacency and delight. While I write this, a very interesting and picturesque group are assembled beneath my window, consisting of the united families of the two gardeners, the *nouvelle accouchée*, and her *bambino*, the grandmother, and some of the neighbours. The children are all touching and kissing the new-born infant, the grandmother cautioning them not to be too rough in their caresses; and the mother, with no symptom of recent illness, *en cheveux*, and dressed *à-l'ordinaire*, is partaking of her usual evening repast, an abundant supply of maccaroni. All seem in high glee, and I am told that to-morrow she will resume her customary occupations, as if nothing particular has occurred.

I should say, judging from the specimens that have fallen immediately beneath my observation, that the Italian peasantry are a very affectionate race. Since I have resided here I have never heard an angry word, or ill-humoured tone of voice from any of the individuals composing the two large families who reside in the *rez-de-chaussée* of this dwelling; but terms of endearment and exclamations of love continually reach my ears from them.

Spent the morning in the Museo Borbonico, and examined the different objects found at Pompeii. They were invested with a new interest to me, from having so lately explored the place to which they appertained. The culinary utensils are so various as those to be met with in the *cuisine* of an aristocratic residence, but infinitely superior in point of design and execution, and each and all more or less ornamented. Loaves of bread with the baker's name still visible on them, with grapes, and other edibles, were shown to us. Various articles for the toilette were also displayed, among which was a pot of rouge, proving that the dames of antiquity were not ignorant of the use of artificial aids for supplying the loss of the roses of health to their cheeks. There are several mirrors of steel in the *museo*, but none of a considerable size. The combs are ill-formed, and look barbarous near the other implements for the toilette; which, for the most part, are prettily shaped, and neatly finished. The lamps far surpass any of those of modern invention. Fancy has given to each some of her most graceful ornaments; and to others, chimeras dire, and grotesque shapes. One was a tree, admirably executed, in the branches of which hung tubes for the oil. The chains of all the lamps were beautiful, and as neatly finished as our gold neck-chains; and none of the lamps were without ornaments, not even those of the most ordinary kind. One article struck me as peculiarly blending the useful and ornamental. It was formed of bronze, and meant to be placed in the chamber of an invalid. It represents a kind of fortress with towers, each of which is formed to contain any liquid intended to be kept warm, and a drawer for burning charcoal fills the bottom of the whole apparatus. This article is so beautifully finished, that it would be an ornament in any chamber, and its utility is obvious. Some of the trinkets in this collection are exceedingly pretty. The gold of which they are composed is very pure, and the designs pleasing, though what we moderns should call *mesquin*, from their slightness and smallness. The rings are generally good, particularly those with

engraved gems, some of which are really beautiful. The armoury
contains helmets, breast-plates, shields and swords, worn by the
Romans, many of them bearing marks of the warfare in which
their owners were engaged; and all in a far less ruinous condition
than the once mighty city, among whose armies they were worn.

9th. – Went yesterday to see the procession of the Fête de St.
Maria Piedigrotta, considered to be one of the most splendid of
the Neapolitan religious festivals. Balconies commending views
of the procession were in great request, and large sums were
demanded for them. The Austrian troops at present occupying
Naples, and amounting to about fourteen or fifteen thousand
men, formed a part of the *cortège*, and added considerably to the
grandeur of its effect. The royal family, followed by the ladies and
officers of the court, filled about forty state coaches, drawn by
eight, six and four horses; and attended by innumerable running
footmen, in quaint, but very rich liveries, wearing black velvet
caps, similar to those of huntsmen. The royal *cortège* was preceded and followed by the troops, and advanced at a slow pace
from the Palace, along the Chiaja, to the Chapel of the Grotto.
The streets were crowded with peasants in their richest costumes, and with *lazzaroni*, more remarkable for the picturesque-
ness, than neatness of theirs. The dresses of the female peasants
of the various districts in the kingdom of Naples might here be
seen; and presented a rich galaxy of the brightest colours, mingled with ornaments of pearl, coral, and gold. The effect was
beautiful, conveying the impression of some vast *bal costumé*,
rather than of the real dresses worn by peasants . . . The carriage
of the King was one surface of highly-burnished gilding. It was
surmounted by plumes of snowy feathers, as were also the eight
horses by which it was drawn. Pages, in the dresses of the olden
times, walked by the side of the carriage, and outside these
moved the running footmen. The rest of the state carriages,
though very gaudy, were shabby and ill-appointed. The ladies of
the court were habited precisely alike, in robes of gold tissue with
broad scarlet stripes; and plumes of feathers, with diamonds in
their hair. The sight of so many ladies similarly attired, conveyed
the notion that they wore a livery, and were literally servants; a
notion that however repugnant to the vanity of courtiers, is
seldom far from the truth.

The ceremony in the chapel occupied not more than twenty

minutes; and the procession returned to the palace in the same order. I was forcibly struck with the difference that marked the conduct of the populace towards the sovereign here, with that which we witness in England to ours. Although the Chiaja was crowded with persons of all classes, not a single huzza or acclamation met his Neapolitan Majesty; nor did his presence seem to occasion the slightest sensation in the minds of his subjects. This indifference is the more remarkable, when we consider the natural enthusiasm, and exuberant animation of this people, and compare it with the habitual calmness of ours. Nowhere have I ever seen a sovereign received with the same demonstrations of affection as in England; demonstrations the more flattering, as proceeding from a free people to their King.

12th. – Went to Herculaneum yesterday, accompanied by Sir William Gell. This excursion may well be called a descent into the grave of a buried city. The noise of carriages rolling over us resembles thunder; and reminds one of active busy life, while thus interred nearly a hundred feet in lava, with the wrecks of past ages. A considerable portion of this city had been laid open, but the excavators, fearful of endangering the buildings in Portici and Resina, erected immediately over Herculaneum, filled up all except a theatre, at present the only vestige open to the inspection of the curious. The *proscenium*, orchestra, and consular seats, with a portion of the corridors, have, even in their present ruinous state, a very imposing effect; and this is heightened by the exclusion of the light of day, the torches throwing a lurid glare on some portions of the building, while others are left in deep shadow. The statues and other ornaments found in Herculaneum have all been removed,[1] and nothing of its former decorations remain, save some arabesques, and portions of *stucco*, painted with a crimson colour of extraordinary richness and lustre. The wild and grotesque figures and animated gesticulations of some guides, waving their torches, which cast lugubrious gleams of light around this sepulchre of a dead city; the dense and oppressive air, and the reverberation of the sound of the carriages, passing and repassing through the streets above it, have an indescribable influence on the mind. One consequently ascends into light and life again with feelings of melancholy,

[1] Now in the National Museum at Naples.

which not even the beautiful scenery that courts the eye can banish for some time.

We spent some hours in the Musuem at Portici, which contains many of the treasures found at Pompeii and Herculaneum. Some of the paintings are very curious, and all are highly interesting. The gods and goddesses of the Pagan mythology, Bacchuses, Bacchantes, nymphs, boys, birds, animals, fishes, and insects, are the general subjects, and are executed with much spirit. But those paintings which represent scenes in the domestic life of past ages, have a superior attraction; hence, a garden, very similar to the Italian gardens of the present day, is beheld with interest; as is a lady looking at herself in a metal mirror; and other groups. One of the most touching mementos of the destruction of Pompeii is here shown, in the impression of a bosom, formed by the materials that destroyed her, whose charms it has thus preserved to posterity. A necklace and bracelets of gold were found with the remains of this young female, and their beauty indicates that she must have been of no mean rank.

19th. – THE MIRACLE OF ST. JANUARIUS. – The miracle of the liquefaction of the blood of St. Januarius, which is exhibited on the 19th of September every year, presents one of the most extraordinary examples of superstition that it is possible to imagine in the present time, when education has so much dispersed the mists of error and ignorance. I witnessed this ceremony to-day, and was little edified by the exhibition. A small portion of the blood of the saint having been preserved by a pious spectator of his martyrdom, it was long after consigned to the custody of the church named after him, of which it constitutes the pride and treasure. It is kept in a vial placed in the *tesoro*, which is a press formed in the wall, with an iron door of great strength, secured by no less than three locks; the keys of which are entrusted to three different bodies of the state, and a deputy from each is sent with its respective key, on the annual occasion of the door being opened. The glass vial which contains the blood is of a circular shape; and the blood beheld through it appears like a morsel of glue. In this state it is exhibited to the spectators, who all examine it. At eight o'clock, mass is celebrated in the different chapels of the cathedral, and at the grand altar, which is mostly richly decorated: a priest officiates, holding the glass vial in his hands, occasionally displaying it to the crowd, and praying with the utmost fervour, and apostrophizing the saint with exclamations interrupted by his tears and sighs. A large wax candle, equal to at least a dozen of our English ones, is placed on the middle of the altar; and I observed that the holy father generally held the vial very near to it.

It was about ten o'clock when we entered the chapel; and as the priest had then been two hours invoking the saint to consent to the miracle, the spectators were becoming very impatient. On the left side of the altar, a place was assigned to about one hundred women, who are said to be descendants of the saint; and therefore have this place of honour on the occasion. When, half an hour after our arrival, no symptom of liquefaction was visible, the cries of these women became really terrific, resembling more the howlings of savages than of Christians. Their shrieks were mingled with exclamations uttered with vehemence, and accompanied with the most violent gestures. They abused the saint in the most approbrious terms, calling him every insulting name that rage or hatred could dictate. Through the influence of a friend we were permitted to approach near the grand altar, where we maintained a gravity that ought to have conciliated the good opinion of the worshippers of St. Januarius: but after his unnatural descendants had exhausted every term of vituperation on him, they began to direct sundry glances of mingled suspicion and rage against us; and at length avowed their conviction that it was the presence of the English heretics that prevented the liquefaction of the blood. The priest made a sign to us to take off our bonnets and to kneel, which we immediately did. This compliance appeased the anger of the relatives of the saint against us; and once more they directed their abuse to him, calling down imprecations on him for resisting the prayers of his descendants. *Briccone! Birbone!* and other terms of abuse were showered on him, for what they termed his obstinacy; but, fortunately for their lungs and our ears, the blood began to liquefy! the vial became filled in the course of two or three minutes after the first symptom of dilution.

No sooner was the fulfilment of the miracle announced than the whole congregation prostrated themselves, and after a few minutes' thanksgiving, gave way to the most lively joy; uttering a thousand ejaculations of love and gratitude towards the saint to whom, only a short time before, they had addressed every term of abuse with which their vocabulary furnished them. Men, women, and children, now began to weep together; and never previously had I witnessed such an inundation of tears. Several soldiers, Austrians as well as Neapolitans, were present in full uniform, and appeared as equally impressed as were the rest of the congregation with the wondrous miracle that had taken place. The vial was paraded about by the priest, and pressed to the foreheads of the pious, who were also suffered to kiss it, a ceremony performed with enthusiastic devotion. During this operation a number of priests, young and old, were industriously plying their vocation of levying contributions on the strangers, who were told, that in honour of the saint and the miracle, it was hoped that they would not deny their charity. A group of juvenile Chinese, who have been sent to Naples to study, and take priests' orders, were most demonstrative in their enthusiastic admiration of the miracle, and their sallow plain countenances were not improved by their smiles and tears. It is melancholy to see super-stition extending itself to such regions as China: and I could not help breathing a wish that these youths had studied religion in a more enlightened school, that they might have carried back to their country the pure principles of Christianity, instead of those of superstition. Whether the liquefaction is produced by some chemical operation effected through the warmth of the hand, or its vicinity to the large candle alluded to, or both, I cannot decide; but I confess I left the spot an unbeliever of the asserted miracle.

In a remote part of the church several priests were going through the ceremony of ordination. They were at an altar, with a large circle, inclosed by a balustrade, at which several dignitaries of the church were officiating. The neophytes were prostrated on the ground, bathed in tears, whether caused by regret for their abandonment of the world, or a sense of their own unworthiness for the sacred profession they had chosen, I could not discover: but their emotions seemed to awaken kindred ones in the crowd of both sexes assembled around the balustrade, and the women, in particular, wept bitterly . . .

October, 1823. – Our old friend, General Sir Andrew Barnard,[1] has been spending some days with us. He is as much delighted with Italy as we are, but must return to England *bon gré mal gré*. This is one of the miseries of being attached to a Court.

[1] General Sir Andrew Francis Barnard (1773–1855) who had been in command of the English troops in Sicily in 1806.

Went yesterday to see the Campo Santo. This cemetery consists of a very large parallelogram, excavated and divided by
masonry into three hundred and sixty-five vaults of great depth,
and having no communication with each other. A massive square
flag covers the opening, which is hermetically sealed; and in this
flag is inserted an iron ring, by which it is raised when required.
These vaults are all numbered, and one is open every day in the
year, for the reception of the dead bodies, from dawn until
midnight, when it is closed. Quicklime is then thrown in, and it is
said that in a short time no trace of the dead, save the bones,
remain, so rapid is the decomposition. At the end of a year, each
vault is re-opened, and made ready for its new tenants, by
removing the bones and skulls, and burning them for the purpose of manure. The cemetery is surrounded by walls on three
sides, and the fourth is occupied by a building with arcades and
benches, for the reception of the dead while the flag is being
raised. No coffins are allowed, and the shells used for conveying
the bodies are brought away. The vault open yesterday was
nearly three parts filled when I looked into it; and never did my
eyes encounter so hideous a sight as it presented! The light of a
brilliant sun fell obliquely into this charnelhouse, throwing its
beams on some portions of the tenants of the vault; while others
were left in deep shadow, like some picture by Rembrandt, but
far more fearful than his pencil ever depicted. The bodies, from
having been thrown in, lay in the most incongruous contact, and
some, in falling, had assumed singularly fantastic positions. Male
and female, the youthful and the aged, were mingled together in
grisly fellowship. An old man, with a long white beard, the
growth of a protracted disease, was covered all save his
venerable-looking head, by the luxuriant raven tresses of a young
female corpse, who had fallen close to him; while her person was
nearly concealed by those of three children, whose limbs, protruded in grotesque attitudes. Heads, feet, and arms were seen
jutting out at different sides, beneath the figures on the top of this
heap of mortality; and what added to the revolting horror of the
scene was, that a number of reptiles were crawling over the dead,
and had already commenced preying on them. The soul shud-
dered, and the mind shrank back appalled from this hideous
charnelhouse. How can any human beings bear to consign their
dead to such an abode! The depths of ocean were a better grave
than this den; where death, while robbed of its solemnity, is

rendered more ghastly, more terrific, and more revolting, by its victim being thrown into disgusting and obscene contact, to rot, and mingle their putridity together . . .

November, 1823. – I have made acquaintance, at the Archbishop of Tarentum's, with many scientific and literary characters; among whom no one has more pleased me than the celebrated Piazzi,[1] the astronomer. His manners are peculiarly agreeable, for though he is remarkably well bred, they possess an originality and racines always interesting, and not often to be met with in a person who has mingled so much in society. He is far advanced in the value of years; but his mind is a vigorous and active as ever. He is tall and slight, his physiognomy very *spirituel*, with an expression of good-nature not generally appertaining either to the character or countenance of those remarkable for their *esprit*. He has been from early youth the friend and companion of the admirable Archbishop of Tarentum. Both philosophers, in the best and truest acceptation of the term, their knowledge of human nature, which is profound, has but induced them to feel a greater degree of forbearance towards the weak and erring, and a livelier admiration for the good. Piazzi is a Sicilian by birth, and a distinguished himself, while yet a child, by a passion for astronomy, which denoted the pre-eminence he was likely to attain in that science. Nor has his progress in it disappointed the expectations formed by his friends; as his discovery of the planer Ceres ranks him among the most eminent of the modern astronomers. The Abbe Monticelli[2] is another of the acquaintances I have cultivated. He is considered the best geologist in Italy; and is remarkably agreeable as well as instructive in conversation.

Few days elapse without our spendin some hours with the excellent and amiable Archbishop of Tarantum, who attracts around him a circle composed of the most enlightened and pleasant people of his own and every other nation. I never saw a man so universally esteemed, and certainly never one who more merited to be so. His love of the fine arts, and encouragement to artists, draw to his house the best specimens of both; and many a

[1] Giuseppe Piazzi (1746–1826). President of the Royal Society of Sciences at Naples and discoverer if the planet Ceres.

[2] Teodoro Monticelli, b. Brindisi 1759, d. Pozzuoli 1845.

one has found patrons through his recommendation, who might otherwise have pined away existence on obscurity.

We see a good deal of the Duc di Rocco Romano,[1] one of the most distinguished Neapolitan generals, and the very personification of a *preux chevalier;* brave in arms, and gentle and courteous in society. There is something really chevaleresque in the bearing of Rocco Romano; and what renders it more attractive is, that it is in perfect keeping with his military reputation. Though said to be nearly sixty years old, he certainly does not look above forty; and is in his person as active as most men of thirty, and as lively as any are at twenty. Time affects people infinitely less in this mild climate than with us. Here I see many persons flourishing at an age that in England would have been attended with most, if not all, the infirmities peculiar to the decline of life; and have observed in them an animation and gaiety seldom to be found even in the youthful in our cold climate.

The Neapolitan ladies are generally handsome, and some eight or ten of them are exceedingly beautiful. Their manners are easy, graceful, and natural; perfectly free from even the semblance of affectation or coquetry. In mixed society they are much more reserved than the ladies of England or France; but this restraint arises, not from prudery, but from a natural timidity and reserve when with strangers. Shaking hands with gentlemen is deemed to be indecorous, even when long acquaintance has existed. In *soirées*, men never presume to sit by a lady, establishing those *têtes-à-têtes* so frequently seen in English society; but advance to the formal rows, or circles, in which ladies are seated, and converse with them, standing respectfully all the time, in terms so purposely audible, that the surrounding persons may hear all that is said. Some portion of the Spanish ceremoniousness may still be detected in the manners of the higher class of the Neapolitans; but this soon wears off, particularly among the women, for the ladies here are peculiarly gentle and amiable to strangers of their own sex.

Sir William Gell is so beloved by the Neapolitans, that any friends of his are received by them with distinguished politeness; and as he possesses the rare tact of knowing the persons likely to suit each other, his introductions are generally productive of pleasure to all parties. Indeed, a most favourable impression of

[1] General Lucio Caracciolo, duca di Roccaromana.

the English exists here, given by the long residence of Sir William Drummond, Gell, and Mr. Keppel Craven at Naples, which has enabled the inhabitants to estimate the many admirable qualities of these gentlemen. Mr. Craven possesses a highly-cultivated mind, manners at once dignified and graceful, and exercises an elegant hospitality, that renders his house among the most attractive here.

My old friend, good, kind Lord Guildford,[1] dined with us yesterday. He is *en route* for England, attended by Heaven only knows how many Greek professors and their wives. Never was a mortal man so devoted to one pursuit, as this estimable creature is to the restoration of literature in Greece. It has become a monomania with him, for he thinks of nothing else, speaks of nothing else, except his college. He has given us a pressing invitation to visit him at Corfu, not so much, I verily believe, for the sake of our society, as for the purpose of showing us his literary establishments. People laugh at this hobby of Lord Guildford's, and think it denotes nothing short of insanity in a British peer, to prefer devoting a large portion of his fortune to the education of the Greeks, to expending it in England in dinners, balls, and *fêtes*, like so many of his class. But such is the wisdom of our times, that all who serve others, or evince a more than ordinary interest in the well-being of their fellow-men, are forthwith suspected of folly. Byron has been mocked for going to fight for the Greeks; Lord Guildford is derided for educating them!

Naples is filling fast, and many English have arrived. As yet we have escaped even the semblance of winter, except the occasional storms that sometimes at night remind us of the season. There has been no day in which we have not been able to ride or drive, as if it were September instead of November; and although we have no fire-place in any of the sitting-rooms which we occupy, we have not suffered from cold. The substitute for fires are *bracieri*, in which a small kind of charcoal, made from the wood of myrtle, is burned; and this dispenses a sufficient warmth, without any unpleasant odour or vapour. These *bracieri*, in shape, resemble an antique vase, or urn, and are made of *terra-cotta*, with the cover pierced. They stand on low pedestals, are generally ornamented with antique designs, and have a classical appear-

---

[1] Rev. Francis, 6th Earl of Guildford (1772–1861).

ance. We find two, sufficient to warm each of our large drawing-rooms, and one, the less. We have experienced no ill effects from the use of the *bracieri*; and by throwing into them perfumed pastilles prepared for the purpose, they emit a very agreeable odour. Notwithstanding that we do not miss the warmth of a fire, we greatly miss the appearance of that truly English focus of comfort, which attracts round its cheerful hearth the domestic circle of a winter's evening; and we all admit that we should prefer encountering some portion of the severity of a northern winter, with a home fire-side, to the mild seasons here, which have led to its exclusion from Neapolitan houses.

Count Paul Lieven,[1] and Mr. Richard Williams have arrived here, and dined with us yesterday. The young Russian speaks English like a native, is exceedingly good-looking, and possesses a quick-ness of perception and discrimination that peculiarly fit him for arriving at eminence in his diplomatic career. Mr. Richard Williams is a good specimen of an Englishman, well-looking and well-bred, with an inquiring, active, and cultivated mind. Both formed a pleasing contrast with the Prince L—, who also dined here, and whose discordant voice still rings in my ears; although, Heaven be thanked! not one of the sentiments it breathed have rested in my memory. A low voice is charming in man as well as in woman; and I never was more convinced of this fact, than after having my ears tortured by the screaming tones *di Sua Eccellenza il Principe* L—.

Lord Ashley[2] and Mr. Evelyn Denison[3] dined here yesterday. I have seldom seen a more distinguished young man than the first. His air aristocratic, yet free from the *fierté*, supposed to accompany *l'air noble*, and his manners manly and dignified. Highly educated, he seems bent on acquiring the knowledge only to be attained by travel, and an acquaintance with other countries, and bids fair to be an ornament to his own. Mr. E. Denison is a remarkably gentleman-like, well informed young man. Sir William Gell, who met them at dinner here, gave them much useful

[1] Son of Prince Christoph Lieven, Russian Ambassador to Berlin 1809–12 and London 1812–34, and his wife, Princess Dorothea Lieven (1785–1857), d. of Count Christoph von Benckendorff.

[2] Anthony, Later 7th Earl of Shaftesbury (1801–1885).

[3] John Evelyn Denison (1800–1873). Speaker of the House of Commons and created Viscount Ossington in 1872.

information about Sicily, to which place Lord Ashley intends proceeding.

Dec. 1823. – As yet we have had no winter here, and no day without more sunshine than is to be enjoyed in England in the midst of summer. This escape from Winter is really a blessing to invalids; and when one is basking in the genial warmth of this sunny clime, and reflects on the snow and sleet that is probably at this moment covering our English shores, it is impossible, even in despite of patriotism, not to admit that Italy is a preferable winter residence. Enjoying the frequent society of Sir William Drummond, Gell, Mr. Craven, Mr. Mathias, and a pleasant admixture of the Neapolitans, with the travellers of all countries who come to Naples, it would be difficult to find a place where time can be more agreeably passed than here. Sir William Drummond and Gell, who have tried so many other places, give this the preference, and by doing so, certainly add much to its attractions. Nor has dainty food been wanting to gratify the palate, while a rich treat has been afforded to the mind. The wild boar, a delicacy much in request here, and the veal of Sorrento, the whitest and most delicious I ever tasted, with well-flavoured poultry, have been abundantly supplied; and our cook has rendered them ample justice by his culinary skill.

Jan. 1824. – The new year has opened most propitiously, for the weather is delicious. The garden here boasts so good a supply of flowers, that one can hardly believe when looking on it, that we are still in the depth of winter, of which we are only reminded by the shortness of the days. We have added many individuals to our list of acquaintances here, some aquisitions as well as additions; among whom may be ranked Signor Salvaggi,[1] a man of considerable literary acquirements, and most agreeable manners.

The Duc de Cazarano [? Casarano] and Marchese Giuliano,[2] were presented to us by the Duc de Rocco Romano, and we see them frequently. Cazarano is a very amusing person, draws well, and is an admirable mimic, and Giuliano has been some time in England, whither he went when Murat lost the Neapolitan

[1] Gaspari Selvaggi (1763–1847).
[2] Marchese di Giuliano is one of the titles held by members of the Rospigliosi family.

throne. The devotion of some of the Neapolitan officers to Murat was very touching, and failed not to the last; and among them, Rocco Romano and Giuliano were distinguished. They are now permitted to live free from molestation here; but have not yet been employed by the present government.

February, 1824. – The carnival has disappointed me: not that it was wanting in the noisy gaiety peculiar to festivals here, but that after the novelty of the first quarter of an hour's view of it had passed away, the repetition of grotesque groups, ludicrous masks, and extravagant costumes, became as fatiguing to the mind as to the eye. The Neapolitans, high and low, rich and poor, enter into the spirit of the carnival, with a reckless love of pleasure and zest, that appertains only to children in other countries. Even the old seem to enjoy the general hilarity produced by the heterogeneous *mélange* of Neptunes, Hercules, Cupids, shepherdesses, sailors, Spanish grandees, and a hundred other absurd masks. Innumerable carriages, filled with these votaries of pleasure, pass and repass in the Strada Toledo, playing their antics, and hurling at the persons they encounter, showers of *bon-bons* and bouquets of flowers. The dress of English sailors seems to be a favourite one with the maskers at the carnival, for we saw several worn by persons whose equipages indicated that they were of the aristocracy. The lower class substitute a composition of plaster of Paris for *bon-bons*, and often throw them with a violence that occasions accidents. Large are the sums expended by the gay Neapolitan gallants, in the purchase of the most delicate *bon-bons* and fragrant bouquets, which they threw into the carriages or windows, where they recognise their female acquaintances. A party of the *noblesse* a year ago, during the carnival, passed through the Strada Toledo, in a ship, placed on wheels, and fired from the guns at each side, volleys of *bon-bons*. Never were broadsides so amicably received, or so agreeably remembered, for they still form the topic of conversation, whenever a carnival is mentioned.

Melancholy news are arrived from Rome, announcing the death of the beautiful Miss Bathurst.[1] This sad event occurred by

---

[1] Miss Rose Bathurst. A monument by the sculptor, Westmacott, was erected in the English Cemetery at Rome and Lady Blessington went to see it on 9 May 1828. The monument was put up by Mrs. Bathurst who

her horse slipping into the Tiber, from a narrow path near its edge, when she attempted to turn him; and though she rose to the surface of the water on horseback, the efforts of the horse in swimming burst the girths, and she was precipitated again into the flood. She rose once more, and then disappeared into its turbid depths for ever, in the presence of her agonized friends, who saw her perish without the power of saving her. A fatality seems to be attached to the family. Her father, a most amiable man, and son to the worthy and esteemed Bishop of Norwich,[1] disappeared some years ago, when travelling in Germany, and was never more heard of, leaving a wife and two infant daughters to lament his loss; and now one of these daughters, in the flower of youth and beauty, is snatched from life, and in a manner, too, that renders the blow still more afflicting. I remember seeing this lovely girl, hanging on the arm of her fond mother, coming out of the Opera, at the close of the season of 1822, and being greatly struck with her appearance. What a new and terrible blow must this event be, to the bereaved wife and mother! It appears that Miss Bathurst, who was residing at Rome, under the protection of her uncle and aunt, Lord and Lady Aylmer,[2] rode out with them, escorted by the French ambassador, the Duc de Laval-

---

wished to have her daughter's figure flying up to Heaven and Mr. Bathurst (who had died earlier) seated on a cloud to receive her. Princess Lieven in a letter to Prince Metternich says that the French Ambassador, the duc de Laval, was present at the accident, but lost his head and bolted across the country till one in the morning.

[1] Henry Bathurst, Bishop of Norwich, 7th son of Benjamin, younger brother of Allen, 1st Earl Bathurst (1744–1837). Bishop of Norwich from 1805.

[2] Matthew, 5th Baron Aylmer (1775–1850) m. Louisa Anne, 2nd d. of Sir John Call, Bart. of Whiteford, Cornwall. A letter from Lord Aylmer (undated and quoted by Maddan) gives a rather different account of the accident: "When at Bath, it did not occur to me to mention to Mr. (Walter Savage) Landor, an error into which Lady Blessington had been led, in her *Idler in Italy*, when describing a certain dreadful event at which Louisa and I were present at Rome. She says that I was prevented by Louisa from rendering any assistance to that Poor girl who there perished, to our indescribable anguish; whereas you know I made two distinct attempts to save her, and was very nearly drowned myself in doing so, more especially in the last, when I gave myself up as lost. Do you think it worthwhile to mention this to Mr. Landor, who is, I believe, in habits of intimacy with Lady Blessington."

Montmorenci. The groom of Miss Bathurst was sent back to the residence of Lord Aylmer with some message; and when the party arrived near the Ponte di Molle, the Duc proposed leading them by a path which he had often previously ridden, along the bank of the Tiber. The river having become swollen, portions of the bank had given way, which rendered the path so narrow, that after pursuing it some short distance, the Duc, who was foremost, proposed retracing their steps. In endeavouring to turn her horse, Miss Bathurst unfortunately backed him too near the edge of the bank, which gave way, and horse and rider were plunged into the river. Not one of the party could swim; nevertheless, Lord Aylmer attempted to rush into the water, and had advanced some paces, when his distracted wife held him forcibly back. What renders this sad catastrophe still more lamentable is, that the groom, who had been sent back to Rome, is a good swimmer, and might have been able to rescue this charming young girl from her watery grave. The letter from Rome which I have read, giving these particulars, adds that a more heart-rending scene was seldom witnessed, than that presented by the horror-stricken group on the border of the river, as they watched the object of so much affection rising to the surface of the river, and then saw her engulfed in its turbid depths for ever, leaving no trace but a wide circling eddy on the water, that quickly disappeared . . .

March, 1824. – The last month has flown away rapidly, and pleasantly, – sight-seeing, making excursions, and cultivating pleasant acquaintances. Never did time seem to pass so fleetly as at Naples; the delicious climate rendering existence so positive an enjoyment, that occupation is seldom felt necessary, as in England, to fill up the hours when bad weather and gloomy skies deny the power of out-of-door amusements. I have explored, on horse-back, all the environs of this gay city, many of the most beautiful ones are only accessible to pedestrians, or equestrians. We have made acquaintance with most of the peasantry, and all their children, whom we encountered in our rides; and are now welcomed by them with kind greetings whenever we appear. Every path through the vineyards, and every Madonna in the little niches erected for their reception on the by-ways we frequent, are become as familiar to us, as the immediate vicinity of Mountjoy Forest;[1] and charming are the landscapes that we have

---

[1] Lord Blessington's estate in Ireland.

seen, by thus leaving the high roads, and wandering through the little hamlets and secluded parts of this enchanting country. In these rambles, we have stopped to converse with many a group of peasants, who have ceased their labours, and the songs which invariably accompany them, pleased to converse with strangers, who evinced kindness towards them. They are the most contented race of people under the sun; for never have we heard a complaint of poverty, notwithstanding that several indications of it were visible. Their labours are cheered by songs and smiles, that lighten, if they do not make them forget them. Here the earth yields its productions to her children, like a profuse and generous mother, instead of, as in colder regions, requiring to be rendered fertile by hard labour. I have seen the ground turned up by the feet alone, the aid of spades or ploughs being deemed unnecessary. Poverty can be felt so severely by this people, as by ours; for their wants are much fewer, and more easily satisfied. The mildness of the climate renders fuel and warm clothing here, – heavy sources of expense to the poor in colder climes, – much less necessary to them; and maccaroni, the chief article of their food, is so low-priced and nutritive, that even the poorest peasants can produce it. Their habits of sobriety are remarkable; and to this may, I think, be attributed their cheerful temperaments, and general good health.

April, 1824. – Naples abounds with English, who have flocked here from Rome, where they have been passing the winter. Among them are my old friends, Lord Dudley and Ward,[1] as clever, amusing, and eccentric as ever, and Lord Howden and his son Mr. Cradock.[2] They dined with us yesterday, and we passed an agreeable evening.

The eccentricities of Lord Dudley increase with age; and sometimes assume so questionable a shape, as to excite doubts of his sanity in my mind. These doubts are not, however, entertained by others, or at least, if so, are not acknowledged; notwithstand-

[1] John William Ward, 4th Viscount Dudley and 9th Baron Ward (1780–1833) Minister for Foreign Affairs under Canning, Lord Goderich and the Duke of Wellington. Later was created Earl Dudley and Viscount Ednam.

[2] Sir John Francis Caradoc (1762–1839). General. Created 1st Baron Howden in 1819 and changed his name from Craddock in 1820: his son, Sir John Hobart Caradoc (1799–1873) was later 2nd Baron Howden.

ing that he exhibits proofs of aberration of intellect, too palpable
not to be noticed. But the truth is, that a man with forty thousand
pounds a year, and willing to give frequent and good dinners,
must be as mad as a March hare, before people will admit that he
is more than <u>eccentric</u>. Lord Dudley thinks aloud, expresses his
opinions of persons and things, not often in a flattering tone, to
the very persons of whom he is speaking, much in the style of the
characters in Madame de Genlis' *Palais de la Vérité*, frequently
producing the most ludicrous effect. As I have known him long
and well, and have perfect faith in his good-nature, I can only
attribute these examples of his *façons de parler*, to *absence d'esprit*,
and not as many of his acquaintance do, to *méchanceté*.

Conversing with a mutual friend on this topic, two days ago,
he declared his conviction that Lord Dudley only affected the
absence of mind, so much commented on, as giving a privilege of
telling disagreeable truths. So much for the defence of friends!

"No, no! he is far from being insane," added —, "He never
throws away his money in buying things he can do without;
never lends a guinea on any pretext whatever; never makes a
present; looks sharply into his steward's accounts, and gives
capital dinners. No, he is not mad, I'll be sworn; only *un peu
original*; and so are many more of our acquaintance."

Lord Howden is a perfect gentleman of the old school, when
good-breeding was an indispensable requisite to form one. And
what a charm good-breeding casts over all who possess it! It is the
true polish that softens asperities, and renders society agreeable.
Mr. Cradock is very good-looking, very well-informed, exceedingly clever, and very amusing when he chooses to be so. He
talks well on most subjects, and is dextrous in handling an argu-
ment, or pointing an epigram, or *bon-mot*. He enters society, as
an experienced gladiator enters the arena where he is to combat,
prepared to use all the weapons, in the use of which he has
acquired a proficiency. If he fail, it will not be from want of
address, but from the want of a due estimate of the powers of his
opponents; an error peculiar to the clever, and the young.

May, 1824. – Mr. George Howard,[1] the elder son of Lord Morpeth, has been staying a few days with us. He is a very superior

[1] George William Frederick Howard (1802–1864), later 7th Earl of
Carlisle. Chief Commissioner of Woods and Forests. His father, the 6th
Earl, was Lord Morpeth in 1824.

young man, with a highly cultivated mind, and a fine understanding. He has all the steadiness of age, without any of its
acerbity; and all the frankness of youth, without any portion of its
indiscretion or self-conceit. It would be difficult to find a more
rational or a more agreeable companion, or one who is more
calculated to captivate good-will and command respect.

SALERNO. – We have made a delightful excursion to Paestum,
which has more than realised our expectations. The route, which
passes by the Soldiers' quarters at Pompeii, offers nothing very
interesting, until two or three miles beyond that ruined city;
when the country assumes a most rich and varied aspect, presenting the most beautiful views. In no part of Italy have I seen
such scenery as on this route, uniting all the charms of woods,
rocks, and mountains, with dilapidated castles, watch-towers,
churches, and convents, so admirably placed as to appear as if
erected as ornaments in the enchanting landscapes. In one part
may be seen the ruins of a fortress, crowning a mountain which
lifts its bleak front on high; while all beneath it is glowing with the
richest vegetation; and at another turn of the road, the spires of a
convent are seen rising amidst woods, whose umbrageous
foliage forms a fine contrast to their snowy white.

We stopped some time at Nocera, the Nuceria of the ancients,
called Nocera dei Pagani, from its having been taken by the
Saracens. It chief attraction is the church of Santa Maria Mag-
giore, supposed by some to have been an ancient temple converted to this pious use; while others imagine it to have been a
public bath . . .

From Nocera to La Cava, the same beautiful scenery presents
itself, and the latter town is superior to most of a similar extent in
the Neapolitan dominion, being well built and clean. The principal street has arcades on each side, which adds much to the
beauty of its appearance, and the inhabitants have an air of
tidiness and comfort. It was among the wild and romantic scenery in the vicinity of La Cava, that Salvator Rosa and Poussin
studied nature in her grandest and most picturesque forms, and
several of the subjects of their pictures may be here discovered.

The entrance to Salerno offers one of the finest views that can
be imagined, Placed at the foot of the mountains of Gragnano,
which are considered among the highest of the Apennines, and
bathed by the blue waves of the Mediterranean, its beautiful Gulf

may be said to rival the Bay of Naples, to which it bears a striking resemblance. The ruins of an ancient fortress, crowning the summit of a steep and rocky mountain, of a pyramidical form, which towers on high as a barrier, to protect the town beneath it, add much to the beauty of the scene; as do three other ancient castles, placed on separate and less elevated mountains in the vicinity, which forms a fine back-ground to the picture. No one who has seen the delicious scenery which this spot presents, can wonder at its having been sung by almost all the poets of the Augustan age; for it still preserves sufficient charms to justify their admiration. At Cumae and Baiae, we look in vain for the originals of those pictures given us by the poets, and for those scenes whose attractions drew the luxurious Romans to their shores. All is changed; for nature, more cruel than Time, has by her revolutions effaced much, if not all, their charms, converting those once lovely scenes into dreary wastes, exhaling pestilential gales around.

Salerno, after the war with Hannibal, having been rebuilt by the Romans, was raised to the rank of a Roman cólony, and the Emperor appointed governors, to whom were intrusted the charge of maintaining the conquests successively achieved in Lucania and Brutium; the governors residing part of the year at Reggio, and part at Salerno. After having suffered all the revolutions to which Italy was exposed in after times, and having been taken and pillaged by the Saracens, Duke Robert Guiscard, in the eleventh century, repaired and beautified it, and for that purpose, removed from Paestum the antique ornaments that decorate the cathedral. The ancient Salerno was celebrated for its schools of medicine, which may be traced up even to the period when in possession of the Saracens and Moors . . .

The cathedral of Salerno having been destroyed by the Saracens, the present building was constructed by the order of Robert Guiscard. The modern repairs have been so injudiciously and tastelessly carried into effect, as to leave few traces of the gothic splendour, which, judging by the pulpit and rostrum, which still retain their original beauty, must have marked it. They are decorated with mosaics, composed of marbles of the rarest kind, the colours so well contrasted, as to produce the most brilliant effect. Two magnificent columns of *verde antique*, have been converted into candelabra, and are placed at each side of the choir; the branches for lights spring from the tasteless modern capitals, which ill assort with the beauty of the shafts. The church contains three antique sarcophagi, ornamented with *bassi-rilievi*,which makes up, in spirit of design and gracefulness of attitude, for their deficiency in delicacy of execution. Two of the sarcophagi represent the triumphs of Bacchus and Ariadne; and the third, which contains the ashes of a bishop, is graced with the Rape of Prosperine, and the pursuit of Ceres in search of her; a most pagan decoration for the sepulchre of a saintly son of the Church! Two vases, of singular beauty, are now used as lustral vases here. On one is represented the arrival of Alexander at Nisa, and the ambassadors beseeching his clemency for the town; and on the other, the pleasures of the vintage.

The court of the cathedral, is surrounded by a peristyle, the columns of which, about thirty in number, have been brought from Paestum. They are of granite, *cippolino*, and white marble, and the capitals by no means correspond with them. Some are of the Corinthian order, and the others a bad mixture of the composite; affording proofs both in design and execution, of the degeneracy of the arts when they were constructed. Beneath the peristyle are placed fourteen marble sarcophagi, some Greek, and the others Roman, of the time of the consuls, ornamented with *bassi-rilievi*. The most remarkable represents the chase of Meleager, which seems to have been a very favourite subject with the ancients, as I have remarked it on numberless sarcophagi. Others have the heads of victims, decorated with garlands of flowers and fillets, well executed.

There is something akin to the ludicrous in seeing antique vases and *tazze*, on which are sculptured bacchanalian orgies and pagan festivals, crowned by modern covers, adorned with images of the impious rites represented beneath. An acquaintance of mine, lately returned from Sicily, saw there a most absurd transformation of an antique marble sphynx into a Madonna, which was effected by placing a crown on the head; but the rest of the figure retains its original character: yet round this monstrosity he beheld a crowd of kneeling votaries!

In the centre of the court of the cathedral is a large antique basin, formed out of one single piece of granite. It is thirteen feet in diameter, and of a very fine form. The present government tried to remove it to Naples, but failed in the attempt; and materially injured one side of the basin in making it.

The Subterranean Church which is immediately beneath the

cathedral, is very richly decorated; being entirely cased, ceiling included, with various coloured marbles of the rarest qualities, which reflect the lamps like mirrors on every side, and produce a most brilliant effect. In the centre of this church, inclosed at the foot of the altar, is the body of St. Matthew, which is preserved with great care. Two bronze figures of the saint are placed near his remains, and are said to be endowed with many miraculous properties. But the object which our *cicerone* seemed to think the most worthy of attention, and to which he led us with an air of mingled awe and pride, was a mutilated fragment of a column, before which he requested us to kneel, an approach our ears to it. We obeyed his wishes, and heard a sound similar to that which is produced by a large shell under similar circumstances; but which the pious father assured us was the noise of the gushing blood of a martyr, who had been decapitated on this broken column. This seeming miracle, so easily explained by the merest tyro in acoustics, it would be here considered nothing short of sacrilege to question; and when one sees the uses to which superstition can be applied, it is easy to perceive why science finds so little encouragement among the priesthood of the Roman Catholic religion.

Salerno possesses many of the disadvantages, as well as the advantages, of Naples. If its bay and the beautiful scenery of its environs, may be compared with those of the Capital, it has also its noise and dirt in a proportionate degree; and the streets in the evening are filled with persons of all ages and sexes, whose loud and discordant voices mingled together, produce a most stunning effect on the ears of a stranger; while the intolerable odours of tobacco and garlic, the inhabitants being exceedingly addicted to the use of both these delicacies, occasion an equally disagreeable effect on his olfactory nerves.

Driven from our walk on the shore, by the noise and stench, we entered a boat, and were rowed over the beautiful bay, which was as calm and pellucid as the smoothest lake. The view of the town, and the mountains above it, from the water, is fine beyond the power of description; and the bright colours of the costumes of the peasantry looked picturesque. The whole scene from the distance was beautiful; so beautiful that it was difficult to imagine it could be the one whence we were only a few minutes previously driven by its intolerable atmosphere of tobacco and garlic, and its noise. One of our boatmen, on hearing me make the

observation, philosophically remarked, that many of the scenes
which looked fair from a distance, were found to be far from
agreeable when reached: a truth that none of us were disposed to
dispute.

The Italian language, so soft and musical when spoken by the
upper classes, loses all its charms, when screamed, rather than
uttered, by the people, and sounds as barbarously as Irish, or
Welsh. Who that has heard it fall meltingly from the lips of a
Fodore, or any of the other *prima donnas* of the Italian Opera, in
recitative, could imagine that it was the same language that
shocks one's ears in all the streets in Italy, where the lower classes
congregate?

From Salerno to Paestum, we saw little worthy of note, except a
distant prospect of Eboli, a nearer one of Persano, a hunting-
place of the King of Naples; and the river Silaro, now called Sele,
remarkable for the petrifying quality of its water. On a plain,
bounded on one side by a fine chain of mountains, and open to
the Gulf of Salerno on the other, stand the temples so deservedly
celebrated; and the first view of which must strike every beholder
with admiration. Nor is this sentiment diminished on approaching them; for the beauty of their proportions, and the rich and
warm hues stamped on them by time, as they stand out in bold
relief against the blue sky, which forms so charming a back-
ground to every Italian landscape, render the spot, even independent of the classical associations with which it is fraught, one
of the most sublime and interesting imaginable. The solitude and
desolation of the country around, where nought but a wretched
hovel, a short distance from the temples, erected for the accomo-
dation of the post-horses of the visitors to Paestum, breaks on the
silent grandeur of the scene, adds to the sublime effect of it. The
blue sea in the distance, and the chain of mountains as blue,
bounding the horizon, complete the picture . . .

We looked in vain for some traces of the roses of Paestum, so
celebrated by the poets of the Augustan age, that they seldom
noticed flowers without referring to them. Virgil, Propertius,
Ovid, Ausonius, and Martial, have praised them; but these
beauties of nature, like all those of art, for which Paestum was
once so noted, have passed away, and nothing but the temples
and a few ruins remain, to attest its former splendour.

The temple of Neptune, the most remarkable as well as ancient
of the three edifices, was the one we first examined. It is built of a

porous stone, which resembles cork, and bears marks of having formerly been coated with cement. A young architect of no ordinary promise, Mr. Charles Mathews,[1] who accompanied us in this tour, measured the temples, and to him, who will, I hope, publish a detailed account of them, I leave minute particulars, contenting myself with a general description. In the temple of Paestum we met Mr. George Howard, Mr. Archibald Macdonald, and Mr. Millingen,[2] celebrated for his antiquarian lore, who gave us an erudite résumé of all that has been known, or supposed to be known, (the latter division being much more voluminous than the former) of the temples, and of Posidonia. I might enrich the pages of my journal, by noting down some portion of the results of his learned epitome; but, truth to say, my mind was so filled by the reflections on the instability of human greatness, to which the sight of these stupendous monuments of antiquity had given birth, that I was more disposed to loiter alone amidst the ruins, than to profit, as I ought to have done, by listening to his details. There was something so solemn and imposing in the view of these temples, that the eye and the mind must be accustomed to it, before one could bestow an adequate attention on the ingenious hypotheses connected with them. When I looked on their proud fronts, which had braved the assaults of time during so many centuries, and now stood rearing their heads to the blue and cloudless sky above them, I could not help smiling at the little groups moving round their base, who looked like pigmies near these gigantic monuments; yet who, forgetful of how many thousands of their race had passed away since these temples had been erected, or even since they had been considered as antiquities, and how many thousands will pass away before they are vanquished by time, were here discussing them as if they, and not the temples were doomed to live for ages to come!

My sombre reflections were interrupted by the arrival of a barouche, laden with visitors to Paestum; among whom were the young and gay, whose joyous voices sounded strangely in the temple, and whose white draperies, seen floating between the columns, had a picturesque effect. I heard sundry allusions to

[1] Charles James Mathews (1803–1878) who at that time was staying with Lady Blessington at Naples. See *Preface*.
[2] James Millingen (1774–1845), classical antiquary who d. at Naples.

the last "delightful ball at Naples," or the pleasant excursion to Pompeii, as the youthful groups passed through the temples; while the more mature were thoughtful, and examined the ruins, as those only whom Time has touched look on objects that remind them of the tyrant's power. There is no sympathy between the very young and gay, and such scenes as those of Paestum – *mais le temps viendra*! . . .

A collation, that would not have shamed the Sybarite inhabitants said to have once possessed Paestum, was spread in the temple of Neptune; to which, after ample justice had been rendered, succeeded a highly international treat, as Mr. George Howard complied with the pressing request of the company to recite a poem, written by him when at college, on the ruins we were then contemplating. The poem was admirable, and so spirited, as to convey an impression, that it must have been written on the spot, and under the inspiration which the actual scene, and not merely a classical description of it, had created. Mr. G. Howard is a highly gifted young man, with a mind enriched by assiduous cultivation, and manners at once open, manly, cordial, and yet dignified. He is calculated to make friends wherever he is known, and to support the noble name he bears, in all its pristine lustre.

We returned to Salerno, where we spent a very agreeable evening. the strangers who joined our party at Paestum, being no less delighted than surprised by the extraordinary facility and felicity with which Mr. Charles Mathews personated different mendicants, who had assailed us with their entreaties for relief, on our route in the morning; and of whom he gave such perfect imitations in the dusk of the evening, that some of the party who had previously bestowed their charity, reproached the supposed beggars for again demanding it in the same day. Mr. C. Mathews has acquired a proficiency in the different patois of the Italian provinces that is quite surprising, especially when we recollect the short time in which it has been attained; and he emulates his father in the Porteus-like versatility with which he can assume any shape he pleases, of which he gives many very amusing examples.

We embarked at Salerno, intending to proceed by sea to Castellammare, where we had sent our carriages to meet us; but a fresh breeze rendered the briny element so uncongenial to some of our party, that we were induced, though at no slight risk of having our boat swamped by the breakers near the shore, to effect a landing near Amalfi. Nothing could be more rich or romantic than the views presented to us, as we glided along the side of this beautiful coast. Steep cliffs crowned by many a convent spire glittering in the sun; ruined towers half covered by ivy; grottos, and caverns formed in the rocks, through which the sea rushed sonorously, and around the entrance to which the snowy sea-gulls were flying, formed pictures that continually reminded one of the sources of the scenery which Salvator so much delighted to paint. At some spot, groups of men were seen, sending down from the giddy steeps, by the medium of ropes, large bundles of wood, to load boats waiting to receive them; and the boatmen displayed no little skill and dexterity in steadying their little vessels while being laden, and rocked by the heavy swell of the sea. Our crew, with their white shirts, short drawers, and scarlet caps, looked like the pictures I have seen of Greek sailors, their bronzed throats, chests, and muscular legs and arms being left uncovered; and their jetty curled locks escaping from the scarlet caps, beneath which their dark eyes flashed with animation. The whole formed a striking scene to those whom the sea left well enough to enjoy it; among which favoured few I was so fortunate as to find myself. But there were among our party some individuals, whose piteous looks and ghastly complexions, proclaimed their incapability of deriving pleasure from the lovely scenery we were passing. In compassion, therefore, to their misery, we turned our boat towards the shore, at about two miles' distance from Amalfi; and had it dragged through a boiling and brawling surf which, luckily for us, owing to the steepness of the bank, was but shallow, although it broke rudely against our boat, and treated our garments rather unceremoniously.

The boatmen of the Neapolitan coast are a bold and hardy race; they row with extraordinary rapidity, singing snatches of their national barcaroles, while they impel the boat along, or bantering each other with a gaiety and vein of comic wit that are very amusing.

We had a delightful walk to Amalfi, stopping on the way to examine a very large manufactory of maccaroni; the extreme cleanliness of which served to remove the prejudices entertained by some of us, with regard to the mode in which this succulent and favourite food of the Neapolitans is made. The partiality of an Irishman for his potatoes, of a Scotsman for his bannocks, or a

Welshman for his leeks, is cold and tame in comparison with the Neapolitan's enthusiastic preference for maccaroni. The promise of an ample supply of it, is the most powerful incentive that can be held out to him. Its very name seems to act as a magical talisman on his feelings, nerving his arm with new force to urge on his boat . . .

Amalfi justifies all the commendations bestowed on it, for the beauty of its situation; but no trace of its former importance remains[1] . . . Notwithstanding that Amalfi is now reduced from a flourishing city to a rural village, it still boasts a church enriched with the usual quantity of marble, gilding, and paintings to be found in all Italian churches; and of which its simple inhabitants seem to be not a little vain. We loitered in this romantically situated spot, exploring its many natural beauties, until chairs, borne on poles, resting on men's shoulders, were prepared to convey us across the mountains to Castellammare. This is the only mode of conveyance to be procured, and, as visitors to Amalfi are "like angel visits, few and far between," we found some difficulty in obtaining a sufficient number of men to bear our large party; four men being required for each chair, with four more to act as a relay when the previous chair-bearers were fatigued.

At first I confess I felt rather nervous at finding myself conveyed rapidly along, elevated on the shoulders of my porters; nor could I conquer the repugnance naturally entertained, at witnessing men performing the functions of horses, or mules; but the gaiety with which the task was undertaken, and the celerity with which it was performed, soon reconciled me to so unusual a mode of travelling. The chair-bearers only requiring the occupants to maintain a perfect equilibrium, advanced in a rapid trot up the steepest mountain tracks, crossed ravines, through which gushed sparkling water; and descended heights that made one giddy to look down, with a velocity, yet surety of foot, that was truly surprising. Songs and jokes enlivened the way, these cheerful men keeping up a continual and exuberant gaiety, that thus manifested itself, and the relays slipping into the places of the tired chair-bearers so quickly, that the person borne was unconscious of the operation.

[1] During the eleventh and fourteenth centuries two great storms broke over Amalfi changing the contour of the coastline. A great part of the ancient city now lies under the sea.

No description can render justice to the beauty of the scenery between Amalfi and Castellammare,[1] one moment offering views of the blue Mediterranean, seen sparkling over the groves and vineyards, between it and the mountains, and the next showing a convent-crowned eminence, rising from a mass of wood, or a ruined fortress standing on some bold projection of rock. The hamlets through which we passed, were exceedingly pictur-esque. Each had its fountain, round which groups of women were filling their classically shaped water jugs, singing, laughing, and chatting the while; their dark hair rolled like those of the antique female statues, and their scanty drapery revealing just enough of their figures to give them the appearance of having furnished the models, of the rural-nymphs we see in some of the pictures of the old masters. They saluted us gracefully, offered some of the sparkling water, whose coldness they praised; and exchanged smiles and pleasantries with our chair-bearers, which, though fraught with gaiety, were free from even an approach to coarseness.

In one hamlet, Gragnano, the women are famed for their beauty, and though prepared to see them more than usually good-looking, they surpassed our expectations. Tall stately, and well formed, with dark glossy tresses, bound gracefully round their heads, flashing eyes, and clear brown complexions, through which a rich crimson mounted to their cheeks; they really were so charming, that I wished to have had a painter on the spot, who could have rendered justice to such admirable subjects for his pencil. The elderly women were for the most part occupied in plying the distaff, or in tending the little sturdy sun-burnt children, nearly in a state of nudity, who were playing around them; and the male inhabitants seemed to be all absent, engaged in agricultural labour, for we scarcely saw any, except some very old men, who were sunning themselves on stone benches before their doors.

We were not sorry to find a good dinner awaiting us at Castel-lammare; after partaking which, we returned to Naples, highly delighted with our expedition, not the least gratifying part of which had been our passage over the mountains from Amalfi to Castellammare . . .

Sir Wm. Drummond has sent me his "Origines", a work

---

[1] The route taken must have been via Agérola.

requiring all the patient research and profound erudition for which he is remarkable. It rarely occurs that a person who devotes so much of his time to literary labours, should be so brilliant a conversationist as is this gifted man. The versatility of his knowledge is really surprising; proofs of which are elicited by every subject to which conversation may turn, "from grave to gay, from lively to severe."

Lord Dudley took us yesterday to see the Villa Gallo,[1] at Capo di Monte, the pleasure grounds of which are quite beautiful; presenting all the varieties of hill and vale, with rustic bridges spanning limpid streams, and grottos of large dimensions offering delicious retreats from the garish and too fervid rays of the burning sun. Many of the plants, to be found only in hothouses with us, here grow luxuriantly in the open air; and, among the trees, the fine cedars are contrasted by a palm-tree of great beauty, which imparts an Oriental character to the picture. Terraces rise over terraces, filled with flowering shrubs, and giving a notion of the hanging gardens of Babylon; and the views of Vesuvius and Naples, seen from them, with the Caudine Forks near Capua in the distance, form a delightful prospect . . .

Lord Ponsonby[2] dined with us yesterday; he has come to Naples from the Ionian Isles, where he has been residing some time. He is well informed, and exceedingly distinguished in his manners and bearing, both presenting a perfect type of aristocratic high breeding. In England, he was, I am told, considered merely as a fashionable and very gentlemanlike man (the terms are not synonymous); and only such perhaps he might have continued to the present hour, had circumstances not induced him to fix his residence for some years in a place where so little temptation, in the way of society offered, that as a defence from

---

[1] Built by the duca di Gallo in 1809 and later bought by the Queen Mother, Maria Isabella, Archduchess of Austria, who m. as his 2nd wife in 1837, Ferdinand II. It was then known as the Villa della Regina, but is now an Orphanage. The architectural structure remains, although an upper floor has been added in recent years.

[2] John, Viscount Ponsonby, G.C.B. (1770–1855). Diplomatist: suc. his father as 2nd Baron in 1806 and was created Viscount Ponsonby of Imokilly in 1839. Minister Plenipotentiary at Buenos Ayres 1826–28, Rio de Janeiro 1828–30, at the Court of Naples June–Nov. 1832 (after returning from a short period in the Ionian Islands), Constantinople 1832, and Vienna 1846–50.

the inroads of ennui, he devoted much of his time to reading; the fruits of which are agreeably visible in his conversation, which, while perfectly free from even the semblance of pedantry, abounds with information, never obtruded, but always available in society.

We returned yesterday from a very agreeable excursion to Beneventum, known to the ancients by the less happy one of Maleventum; to which name, however, nothing is observable in its site or air to entitle it. Mr. George Howard accompanied us. The route to this ancient city passes through a country not less remarkable for the beauty of some parts of its scenery, than for the interesting souvenirs attached to them . . .

We were very much incommoded by the dust which penetrated into the carriage, in spite of having the glasses, with one exception, drawn up, and literally covered our garments; until no trace of their original tints could be seen, and half blinded and suffocated us. The costume of the women along the route was singular, and more picturesque than neat. It consisted of a roll of linen bound round their heads, and mingled with their long dark tresses; while a scanty drapery, which could not be called a petticoat, as it was open before, and met by an apron, scarcely concealing the coarse chemise, whose corsage shaded the bosom, completed the dress.

It was fortunate that we had sent on our courier the previous day to Beneventum, to prepare a domicile for us; for the town contains but one inn, and private lodgings are out of the question. Some notion of the *agrémens* of this said inn may be formed when I state that the only approach to the *premier étage* was through a stable, filled with horses and bullocks, where a rough staircase, resembling a ladder, enabled us to reach the rooms prepared for us; and which, as might be expected, were strongly impregnated with the odour of the stable beneath them. Palchetti, our courier, had achieved wonders in this miserable dwelling, for he had arranged a room in it to serve the double purpose of *salle-à-manger* and *salon*, by dismissing from it not less than six beds, and white-washing the walls. But notwithstanding this salutary precaution, he had not been able to get rid of the animated inhabitants of the banished beds; for quantities of them might be seen hovering around, and not a few were hopping over the white-washed walls. There was no glass in the windows in this, the only inn of the famed Beneventum; so that no choice remained but that of sitting in darkness by closing the shutters, or freely admitting the air, by having them open, which last alternative we adopted.

Our dormitories did not shame our *salon* by the comfort of their arrangements. Iron frames, on each of which was laid a sack, filled with the straw of Indian corn, with a large pillow *en suite*; two wooden chairs, a table, and two jugs of water, formed the contents of each chamber. A looking-glass, of even the smallest dimensions, was not to be procured; but, thanks to well supplied *nécessaires*, we managed to dispense with the aid of our hostelry. It was also fortunate that we had brought with us a plentiful stock of provisions, for the inn could offer nothing but lean beef resembling horse-flesh, eggs that looked anything but fresh, and potatoes so stinted in their growth, as to prove that they were an exotic luxury.

Beneventum stands on an eminence, beneath a lofty chain of hills, and is washed by the river Calore, over which is a bridge, that constitutes a great ornament to the town. The triumphal arch of Trajan, forms one of the gates of entrance to Beneventum; it is composed of marble, and consists of a single arch. Its sides are enriched by four Corinthian pillars, placed on pedestals, and the interior and exterior are covered with well executed *rilievi*, representing the achievements of the emperor. Although this arch is generally admired, it falls short of my expectations. The sculpture looks meagre, and is fatiguing to the eye to contemplate; yet, as one of the best preserve monuments of antiquity in Italy, it offers a very interesting object to those who, like me, love to dwell on such sights.

Near a mill, in the outskirts of the town, some huge fragments of stone, said to be the remains of an ancient bridge, were pointed out to us, of which the miller seemed not commonly proud. This pride in the wrecks of former splendour, is peculiar to the Italians; who having little in the present to boast of, save their delicious climate and beautiful country, turn with complacency to the remnants of their past grandeur.

The Cathedral is of large dimensions, and is a mixture of the Gothic and Saracenic style of architecture, which produces a good effect. It contains an abundance of white marble columns, said to have belonged to antique temples in the neighbourhood; but has little else to recommend it to attention.

As we sauntered through the town of Beneventum, we

observed several persons entering a church, into which we also bent our steps, and witnessed one of those exhibitions so common in Italy; where the enthusiasm and passionate warmth of the preachers, so frequently lead them to overstep the propriety of their calling, the matter of the sermon and manner of this expounder of the Roman Catholic Faith, were truly surprising, and to say the truth, not a little shocking to our feelings, although the rest of the congregation evinced great admiration, for what to us appeared so *outré* and indecorous . . .

We stopped to see Caserta,[1] on our route to Beneventum. It reflects credit on the munificence of Charles III., and on the architectural taste and skill of Vanvitelli; and is justly accounted the most magnificent residence of which any sovereign is possessed. The portico which forms the entrance is above five hundred feet in length, and the staircase is the finest imaginable. The chapel is very beautiful, and the theatre is positively splendid. But the aqueduct, though I saw it only from a distance, attracted my admiration more than the palace, fine as it is. Nothing can form a more beautiful picture in a landscape; and as a mere object of beauty, without reference to its utility, it forms a suitable appendage to a palace . . .

We ascended Vesuvius a few days ago, accompanied by our amiable friend, Sir William Gell. Nothing could be more propitious than the weather; the atmosphere being of its usual clearness, and the air unusually cool and refreshing. We left our carriages at Resina, and entered the house of San-Salvador, the most esteemed of all the guides to Vesuvius, while the asses, who were to bear us to the hermitage, were getting ready for the expedition. From the window of Salvador's dwelling a scene presented itself worthy of the pencil of Hogarth,[2] and to which his alone, or that of the admirable Wilkie,[3] on whom his mantle has descended, could have rendered justice. To convey our party, which consisted but of eight, sixteen asses attended by thrice as many men and boys, followed by their mothers, wives, sisters, daughters, and aunts, were assembled; all and each anxious that the ass or asses belonging to their family should be engaged, and

[1] One of the most magnificent royal palaces in Europe. Was begun by Charles III in 1751 from plans by Vanvitelli, and after his death in 1763, was completed by his son Charles.

[2] William Hogarth (1697–1764). Painter and Engraver.

[3] Sir David Wilkie (1785–1841). Painter.

vociferating loudly the most hyperbolical commendations of theirs, and the most unqualified abuse of the animals of their competitors. The dresses of this animated group, were composed of the gaudiest colours, and were sufficiently tattered to satisfy the most ardent admirer of the picturesque.

Salvador having selected eight of the most promising looking asses, we proceeded to mount our patient steeds; but we found this no easy operation to effect, owing to the angry violence of the rejected ass proprietors, who assailed the accepted ones, not only with torrents of abuse but with sundry blows, from which the gentlemen, and servants who attended us, had great difficulty in shielding our persons in the *mêlée*. The donkeys on which we were mounted, came in for several of the blows aimed at their owners; and became so restive in consequence, that we could scarcely retain our seats. The women and girls took an active part in the fray, loading the rival factions with the bitterest invectives: and, suiting the action to the word, laid violent hands on each other's drapery and headgear. Although exposed to the chance of sharing the blows meant for our donkey-men, the whole scene was so irresistibly comic, that personal fear was forgotten in the laughter it excited.

At length we escaped from our assailants, and proceeded on our route to the hermitage; which, for the first mile, passes through vineyards. Our guide pointed out to us the villa of *Mi Lor* Grandorge (sic), a very respectable English shopkeeper established at Naples, but whom the peasants honour with the designation of "Mi Lor" – a custom peculiar to this country. Sir William Gell asked them, "how it was that they imagined a grand English lord could keep a shop and serve his customers," when one of them answered that "he knew all the English nation kept shops, which made them so rich." This was a curious coincidence with Napoleon's opinion that "the English were a nation of shopkeepers."

After a tedious, though not disagreeable ascent of about three or four miles, over different strata of lava and *scoriae*, each turn in our route offering us the most beautiful views, we arrived at the hermitage, to which we were welcomed by the peal of the bell, just then ringing for prayers. Its measured chime, unbroken by any other sound, with the wide expanse of sea and land spread out beneath us, had a solemn effect; while the sterile mountain above, on a ledge of which we stood, with its blue smoke circling towards the sky, seemed as a beacon to warn us of the destruction it might spread over the beautiful scene upon which we looked. The hermitage stands on a ridge of the mountain; and is so situated that, in an eruption, the lava rushes down in torrents at each side of it, through channels formed by former eruptions, without injuring this quiet abode, which resembles a simple farm-house. This dwelling is sheltered by a few trees, which in so barren a spot, appear to singular advantage; and is inhabited by two hospitable monks, who "spread their simple store", and press and smile, offering all the refreshments within their limited means to those who call at the hermitage. The view from the stone bench in front of this house is indescribably beautiful; and while enjoying it, the monks approached with biscuits, and some of the *Lachryma Christi*, which they strongly recommended us to taste, to prepare us for the ascent . . .

Having refreshed our donkeys at the hermitage, we again pursued our route along the ridge on which it stands; until we reached the commencement of the very steep ascent, where we were compelled to quit them, leaving Sir William Gell at the hermitage. It was curious to observe a party who were on the summit above us, and who appeared like fairies, their small, dark speck-like figures seen against the bright azure of the cloudless sky that bounded the horizon. Chairs, resembling those used in English farm-houses, and, suspended to poles in a similar way to those that conveyed us across the mountains from Amalfi, were here ready for our use. But having tried one of them for a short time, I found the movement so disagreeable, owing to the chair-bearers slipping, and falling down at nearly every second step, in consequence of the lava and *scoriae* crumbling beneath their feet, that I preferred descending from my unstable altitude. Assisted by the arm of Salvador, and holding by leather straps fastened round the waist of one of the guides who preceded me, I managed to ascend; but not without considerable difficulty and fatigue; being, like Sisyphus in his task, rolled back at each step, and at each step carrying away loose fragments of lava, gravel, and cinders.

A most piteous sight was presented to us by the ascent of a very fat, elderly Englishman, who commenced this painful operation at the same time that we did. He was, like me, preceded by a guide with leathern straps, to which he adhered with such vigorous tenacity, as frequently to pull down the unfortunate man, who complained loudly. The lava, gravel, and cinders, put in motion by the feet of his conductor, rolling on those of the fat gentleman, extorted from him sundry reproaches, to which, however, the Italian was wholly insensible, not understanding a word of English. The rubicund face of our countryman was now become of so dark crimson, as to convey the idea of no slight danger from an attack of apoplexy; and it was bathed, not in dew, but in a profuse perspiration, which fell in large drops on his protuberant stomach. Being afraid to let go the leather straps for even an instant, he was in a pitiable dilemma how to get at his pocket handkerchief. Panting and exhausted, he used a considerable portion of the breath he could so little spare, in uttering exclamations of anger at his own folly in attempting such an ascent; and in reproaches and "curses, not loud but deep," on the stupidity, as he termed it, of his guide. He had not less than eight or ten falls during the ascent; and at each fresh disaster bellowed like a bull, which drew peals of laughter from the chair-bearers and guides. One of our party offered to take out his pocket handkerchief, seeing how much he stood in need of it; an offer which he thankfully accepted, but explained that his pocket was secured by buckles on the inside, to prevent his being robbed . . .

On arriving at the summit of the mountain, the view of the sea and land around was so beautiful, that it was impossible to turn our eyes for some time on the object of our visit, the crater. When we did, the fearful contrast it presented to the enchanting scenery beneath, was truly striking. This vast and yawning abyss was sending up a dense smoke, and many parts of it bore evidence to the smouldering fire concealed beneath its surface, by emitting small though lurid flames. When viewing this immense gulf, and reflecting on the destruction it has occasioned, overwhelming cities and towns, and laying waste the most fertile and beautiful lands, it is impossible not to feel a sentiment of awe; and one cannot divest oneself, at least I could not, of a presentiment that in this smouldering crater, I beheld the engine of future destruction to the enchanting country around. No wonder that it presents so deep and vast a concave, when the substance that once filled this immense and burning bowl, has not only hurled ruin over the cities in its immediate neighbourhood, but has been scattered even to remote countries. A stick thrown down became ignitied in an instant, and the shifting movement of the substance that lines this gulf, one moment bursting into lurid flames, and the next sinking into a dense smoke, conveys the impression that its volcanic properties are still in activity . . .

It is extraordinary that a phenomenon, offering so rich a subject to the imagination of the poet, should not have been seized on by any of those gifted beings, who have immortalized some of the places in its vicinity. The few who have named it, have noticed it only for its fertility, or salubrity; but its horrors, the peculiar province of the poet, have been left untouched. But though poesy, however, has not taken advantage of this wonder of nature, superstition has; for in an account, written A.D. 1062, by Pietro Damiani, we find that the mountain was, in his time, viewed as the abode of super-natural beings, and the place of final punishment for the wicked. He relates many terrific tales on this subject; and asserts, that on the death of any distinguished sinner, the flames burst forth with renewed vigour, as if fed by the fresh fuel afforded by the dead. The use to which so fertile a source of terror might be turned, in a country where superstition is encouraged by the wily and designing, as certain means of producing them power and emolument, was not neglected. When we view the various examples, with which a residence in Italy daily furnishes us, of the gross ignorance, and almost heathenish superstition of the lower orders, even at present, some idea may be conceived of the terrors inflicted on them by so powerful an engine as this volcanic wonder formed, when directed by those in whom they reposed unbounded confidence, and pointed, with unerring aim, at their most vulnerable part.

Our learned countryman, the late Sir William Hamilton, has published an account of Vesuvius[1] that will be read with interest by all who wish for information on the subject: and in the admirable work on Pompeii, by Sir Wm. Gell and Mr. Gandy, whence I have derived much information, many particulars will be found.

A chasm of considerable size, which emitted fire, and lava in a state of fusion, during a former eruption, is still open, and sends up a small column of smoke . . .

With what delight does the eye turn from the contemplation of the fearful and yawning crater, to dwell on the glowing picture seen from the summit of Vesuvius! The bright blue sea, on whose

[1] *Observations on Mount Vesuvius, Mount Etna and other Volcanoes in a Series of Letters addressed to the Royal Society*, London, T. Cadell, 1774. See also B. Fothergill: *Sir William Hamilton. Envoy Extraordinary*, London, Faber & Faber, 1969.

glassy bosom innumerable white sails are flitting, like snowy-pinioned birds; the vine-clad hills and fertile Campania, with the undulating line of the coast reaching out like a crescent towards each end of the Bay; the Isle of Caprea, shielding it from the rude winds or waves of the ocean; and Naples descending to the extreme edge of the shore, as if to lave her terraced palaces in its pellucid waters. The promontory of Misenum lifts its head to the right, and the high land of Sorrento bounds the left; Nisida, Procida, and Ischia are seen rising from the calm bosom of the sea like islands called into life by the wand of enchantment; and all this lovely scenery is bathed in an atmosphere so transparent, and canopied by a sky so heavenly blue, that it looks as if it were indeed, what the Neapolitans proclaim Naples to be, "A piece of Paradise dropped on earth."

The descent from Vesuvius is a much less difficult operation than the ascent; and we achieved it, supported on each side by a guide, with a velocity that really surprised me. We encountered the fat old gentleman, panting and puffing, the perspiration literally falling from his crimson face over his garments, and his guide looking nearly as much exhausted as himself. He tried to speak, but so rapid was our course, that his words were lost in the air; But his rueful countenance fully expressed the state of his feelings.

We found Sir William Gell, and a homely repast, awaiting us at the hermitage; and hunger lent a flavour to the simple fare that the most luxurious collation often wants. During our dessert of apples, we amused ourselves with reading the albums of the hermitage, in which the visitors are requested to write their names, with any observation that Vesuvius, or the hermitage, may have suggested. We found, on an average, twenty English to one of any other nation; and, I regret to add, that the style, grammar, and orthography of the generality of the inscriptions, were not calculated to impress a high opinion of the diffusion of knowledge, or the march of intellect, of which we hear so much in our country. Some French tourists had written severe comments on the inscriptions of the English; and, with illiberality too often practised, applied their strictures to the whole nation, for the vulgarity and ignorance of the few writers in the album of the hermitage. Voltaire observed, that *"Le caractère d'un peuple est souvent dementi par les vices d'un particulier."* This is England judged by the disgust, excited by some of the worst specimens of her inhabitants. Foreigners cannot, or at least, do not understand, that persons may be rich enough to encounter the expenses of making a tour, without being sufficiently educated to derive any advantage from it. Travellers of their countries are confined to persons who possess at least enough cultivation to pass current, without any exhibition of the gross vulgarity so often witnessed in ours, who, belonging to all classes, are, not infrequently, anything but creditable to their country . . .

This day the melancholy intelligence of the death of Lord Byron[1] reached us. Alas! alas! his presentiment of dying in Greece, has been too well fulfilled – and, I used to banter him on this superstitious presentiment! Poor Byron! Long, long will you be remembered by us with feelings of deep regret! This sad news has thrown a gloom over us all. We have been recalling to memory every word, every look of his, during our last interview. His little gifts of friendship to each of us, the tremulousness of his voice, the kind words, the eyes filled with tears – all, all are now remembered, as if it was only yesterday that we parted! And but eleven fleeting months have glided away since we left him; we confidently counting on seeing him again, and he, shaking his head, and with a mournfully prophetic look, declaring his conviction that we should never more meet.

There are moments, when I can hardly bring myself to think that Byron is indeed gone for ever: his looks, his voice, are continually in my recollection, ever since I yesterday heard of his death. A thousand circumstances, trifling in themselves, but associated with our *séjour* at Genoa, and constant intercourse with him, are recurring to memory. I have been reading over the notes of his conversations with me; and could almost fancy, in those well-remembered accents of his, I heard his lips utter the words noted down. How much do I now regret not having fulfilled my promise of writing to him! a promise so earnestly urged on his part, and the non-performance of which now rises up to reproach me for this seeming unkindness.

It is gratifying to witness how generally lamented Byron is here: the Italians mourn him, as if he belonged to their sunny

[1] Lady Blessington met Lord Byron during her visit to Genoa in April–May 1823, but they never saw each other again. Her *Conversations with Lord Byron* are recorded in *The Idler in Italy* in that part of her journal when she was resident at Genoa.

land; and the place where, and the cause for which he died, increase their respect and regret. What glorious works might we not have expected from the maturity of such a genius, when the fountain that supplied it was no longer troubled by the passions, over which experience and reason were gaining a salutary empire. [For Lady Blessington's Poem *On the Death of Lord Byron* see *Appendix B.*] At thirty-seven, Byron had acquired a self-control, and a distaste for the luxurious indulgences to which to many of even a more advanced age give way, that was surprising as it was praiseworthy; and his mind, released from the thraldom of the senses, was every day making a rapid progress towards that elevation, to which those who best knew him felt certain he would ultimately arrive. Had a lengthened span of life been granted to him, he would have yet nobly redeemed the errors of his youth, and left works that would have won a pardon for some productions, which all who esteemed him must regret he never wrote.

Sir William Gell, who was well acquainted with Byron some years ago, is one of the English here who most regret him. He fully understood the character of this wayward and spoiled child of genius, who, favoured to excess by the Muse, was most scurvily treated by the greater part of his contemporaries, and lashed into satire by the scorpion whips of envy. He has escaped from his enemies now, and sleeps well – insensible to the arrows that detraction never ceased to aim at him, he can no more be wrung by seeing the bitterness with which the envious, a mighty host, pursued him; and that acute sensitiveness, the peculiar attribute of genius, and which forms at once its power and its curse, can no longer be tortured by the malignity, that for years repaid the delight afforded by his poems, by the most envenomed hostility towards the poet. Who would not tremble at the possession of genius, if hatred and vituperation be its reward; and that such is the case, how many examples may we not find in the lives of the most gifted? Who among the brightest ornaments of our literature, has escaped the malevolence of envy? This reflection is consolatory for mediocrity, for better were it to be denied the distinction which genius can confer, than to pay for it at the price of hatred and detraction.

Dined yesterday with the dear good Archbishop of Tarentum, and met some very agreeable people. In the evening several persons, of both sexes, were added to the party. No one ever did

the honours of a house so admirably as this excellent and venerable man. He has the happy art of making every guest feel
perfectly at ease, and of drawing out the information of each,
with a tact peculiarly his own.

There is something very interesting, in forming one of a circle,
composed of individuals of every land, where each possesses
the good breeding and knowledge of the world, so essential
to the harmony of society; and are influenced by that desire to
please, which half achieves its object. Every one seems amiable at
the archbishop's, even —— ceased to contradict, and —— to
grumble. What a proof, of the salutary influence of the host!

Russians, German, French, Italian, and English, might all be
heard spoken in the same *salon,* last evening, when the visitants
were scattered in groups examining the various objects of taste
and *vertù* that ornament the apartment. But when his guests
assemble round the chair of the dear archbishop, French or Italian
is alone spoken, and his opinions delivered with that suavity
which constitutes so great a charm, are listened to with a respect-
ful deference due alike to his age, character, and superior understanding.

June 1824. – Byron is continually recurring to my memory –
strange, that while he lived, I thought of him but rarely; yet now,
he mingles with every thought . . . [For a second Poem on Byron
see *Appendix* B.]

One of the most agreeable persons at Naples is the Honourable
Mr. K. Craven, and his society is consequently much sought
after. To a great versatility of knowledge, he unites most graceful
manners, considerable skill in music, and performs, as I am told,
in genteel comedy, equal to some of the best professional actors.
He is universally respected at Naples and he, and his *fidus
Achates*, Sir William Gell, are so popular with the Neapolitans,
that they have impressed them with a favourable opinion of their
compatriots, and disposed them to extend their civility to all
recommended to their notice. Sir William Drummond, Sir William Gell, and Mr. K. Craven, having fixed their residence at
Naples, render it still more attractive to English travellers; who
find their houses the most rational society, including distinguished foreigners and Italians, as well as good supplies of
books. We are so fortunate as frequently to see these amiable and
gifted persons, particularly the two first, for Mr. Craven's exemp-

lary attention to his mother, the Margravine of Anspach,[1] who is in delicate health, keeps him much more at home than his friends could wish; but few days pass without our enjoying the society of Sirs William Drummond and Gell. Mathias, too, comes to us frequently, and "God blesses his soul" at every new dainty which our French cook prepares. Two days ago, when he last dined here, this said cook encaged a poor goldfinch in a temple of spun sugar, as an ornament for the centre of the table, for the third course; and the poor bird, while the *convives* were doing honour to the *entremets*, and *sucreries*, fluttered through the temple and beat his wings against its sugary pillars, till they were encrusted with its clammy substance: all which time, Mr. Mathias kept exclaiming, his mouth filled with sweets, "God bless my soul, how strange, how very odd! I never saw a live bird, a real bird in that sort of thing before. Bless my soul, it is very pretty, very curious, indeed; and must have been very difficult to manage." A young child could not have been more pleased with the sight, than Mathias was; and he went away fully impressed with a high opinion of our cook's abilities.

Mr. J. Strangways,[2] the brother of Lord Ilchester, and Mr. H. Bailie, two new arrivals at Naples, dined here yesterday – both well-informed, well-bred, and very agreeable. The young men of the present day, judging from those I see here, are very superior to the race of beaux whom I remember some seven years ago, with little claim to distinction, except the cut of their coats, or the

[1] Elizabeth, Countess of Craven who m. as her 2nd husband in 1791 Christian Frederick Charles Alexander, Margrave of Brandenburg and Anspach. She died at Naples in 1828.

[2] John George Fox-Strangways (1803–1859), half-brother of Henry Stephen, 3rd Earl of Ilchester. Diplomatist of whom Sir W. Gell in a letter to Mr. R. Hamilton, Secretary to the Society of Dilettanti, on 1 May 1833 from Naples: "When Mr. Strangways returned to Naples as Secretary of Legation from Florence, the King asked him on his presentation if he had ever been here before. He replied, 'Yes, with Monsieur Hamilton'. 'Oh Ho', said the King, 'that was a long time ago indeed if you were here in the time of Sir William Hamilton. You will find it all new to you.' The archaic appearance of Strangways put this into His Majesty's head, and occasioned much mirth, as Mr. Hill had always called him, 'old father Strangways with his icicle nose and Mother Shipton hat, looking for daisies and daffodils under a hedge.' He is now gone to Vienna and notwithstanding his seeming antiquity we have lost a very aimable and agreeable person."

tie of their cravats. The march of intellect has effected great changes; and a young man of family, now-a-days, would be ashamed of the mediocrity formerly so prevalent. This promises well for England. Nor do the young Englishmen who come to Italy, abandon themselves to the temptations of this luxurious capital, or indulge in the delicious habits of the *dolce far' niente*, which the climate disposes people to do. Those whom I know, read attentively, compare places with the descriptions given to them in history, and make themselves well acquainted with the policy of the country, its laws, and constitution. They acquire much useful information to fit them for a future career of utility in the senate at home; and I have seen scarcely one, who does not give the promise of proving excellent citizens to old England.

The Duke of Roccoromano and Prince Ischittelli[1] dined with us yesterday. The former is full of anecdotes, and recounts them with a peculiar grace and vivacity; a better specimen of an Italian gentleman could not be found; Well-informed, dignified yet lively, and with a profound deference in his manner towards women, that reminds one of the days of chivalry. Though advanced in years, (report states him to be sixty), his military bearing, and the elasticity of his spirits, give him the appearance of being at least twenty years younger. He was, in his youth, considered to be the flower of the Neapolitan nobility; and innumerable are the conquests he is said to have achieved among the susceptible hearts of his fair countrywomen.

The Neapolitans are, for the most part, highly accomplished. Many of them, of my acquaintance, are good musicians, and draw well; and some compose pieces of music that would not discredit a professor. The talent for versification is much and successfully cultivated amongst them; and I have read many poetical compositions of theirs which, if breathing not the elevated character of genius, were gracefully and elegantly turned. Their epigrams are lively and pointed, and their satires are pungent and terse.

There are many ladies in Naples, remarkable for the grace of their manners, the vivacity and piquancy of their conversation, and their rare skill in music. A *naïveté*, resembling that of children, but wholly free from *brusquerie*, or *gaucherie*, is a peculiar trait in the Neapolitan women; and, in my opinion, gives an

---

[1] F. Pinto y Mendoza, principe d'Ischitella.

additional charm to their society. They are reserved in their intercourse with strangers, until a lengthened acquaintance removes this constraint; when their liveliness, good nature, and sweetness of temper, never fail to endear them to those who have opportunities of knowing them.

I have nowhere witnessed such a perfect freedom from vanity or coquetry, as among the women here; scandal and slander are vices unknown to them; and they consider an indulgence in them so indicative of a bad heart, that they carefully avoid those who give way to this baneful propensity. I have frequently been asked, "Why do the English people tell such ill-natured stories of each other? If founded in truth, they ought, from a patriotic feeling, to be concealed from the inhabitants of other nations; and if untrue, how dreadful to propagate them! But the English seem to relate such tales with a spiteful pleasure, rather than with regret for the crimes they disclose." Such was the observation of a Neapolitan woman, of high rank and cultivated mind addressed to me a few days ago; and sorry was I to find, that this besetting sin of my compatriots, the love of scandal, was so well known wherever they sojourn.

Mr. Millingen, the antiquary, has taken up his abode with us for some days; and has been initiating us into the mysteries of numismatics, a very interesting science, and the study of which serves admirably to illustrate history. The number of false medals offered for sale to collectors, renders a knowledge of the ancient ones very necessary; and so accurate is Mr. Millingen's practised eye, that it can detect a counterfeit at the first glance. Some connoisseurs assert that they can discern the true from the false medal, by the taste; a criterion, in my opinion, to be avoided, as a contact with the verdigris which incrusts them, must be dangerous to the tongue. It is amusing to observe how deeply engrossed each antiquary is by his own peculiar studies: one talks of nothing but Nola vases, seeming to think that they alone are worthy of attention; another confines his observation to antique gems, and will spend hours with a magnifying-glass, examining some microscopic engraving on a precious stone; hazarding innumerable conjectures relating to the subject, and founding some fanciful hypotheses on each. Then comes the lover of mutilated sculpture, who raves of some antique horse, as if it had acquired value by the loss of its limbs; and who admires half a Venus more than an entire one. The connoisseur of *antique bijouterie* must not be forgotten, who pays extravagant prices for golden dropsical Cupids, plump Bacchuses, and lanky Venuses of Lilliputian dimensions, and is as vain of their possession as if he owned the *chefs-d'oeuvre* of a Phidias or Praxiteles. Each of these antiquarians looks down with a pity, bordering on contempt, on the object of the pursuit of the others, believing his own to be the only one meriting devotion; but each, and all, deride him who, attaching himself to the *vertù* of the *cinque cento*, can be pleased with the fine specimens of coloured glass, the beautiful *bijouterie* of Benvenuto Cellini, or the countless other beautiful objects belonging to that epoch. This "onesidedness" of mind, as the Germans would term it, is peculiar to those who allow themselves to be wholly engrossed by one branch of a science, instead of taking a general interest in all; and constitutes the ridicule which these enthusiasts are accused of throwing on such subjects. Mr. Millingen is one of the few antiquarians who is exempt from this defect; for he appreciates, at their just value, every object of art handed down to us from antiquity.

Dined on board our yacht, the Bolivar,[1] yesterday, in the cabin, where Byron wrote much of his Don Juan; a poem, which all who liked him, must wish he never had written. How forcibly inanimate objects remind us of those past away for ever! The table at which he wrote, the sofa on which he reclined, and the different articles of furniture, all in the places where they stood when he owned the yacht, brought Byron back to my recollection most vividly. He was very partial to this vessel, which was built for him at Leghorn, and enjoyed a sail in it very much.

The view of Naples from the bay is beautiful. It presents an amphi-theatre of houses rising one above the other, with a mixture of foliage that adds much to its picturesque effect. The coloured tiles with which many of the churches are roofed, with the minarets, seen in fine relief, against the blue and cloudless sky, give the place the air of an Eastern city, while the tranquil bay, rendering the movement of the vessel scarcely perceptible, enables one to enjoy the lovely picture spread before us.

[1] Maddan states this yacht was built in the arsenal at Genoa for Byron and was later purchased by Lord Blessington. The yacht's captain, Smith, remarked, "this schooner turned out afterwards to be a very full sailer."

August, 1824. – Mr. Herschel,[1] our English astronomer, dined here yesterday, and accompanied us in the evening to the observatory at Capo di Monte, where we were much delighted by the observations we were enabled to make on the heavenly bodies, and still more so by those which he offered; observations which a Neapolitan astronomer, who was present, asserted to be almost as luminous as the brilliant objects that called them forth. Mr. Herschel is a very superior man, and, what all superior men unfortunately are not, a very agreeable one; uniting to a profound knowledge, a fine imagination, and extensive information. What greatly pleased me was his love of poetry, and general acquaintance with our best authors. His *savoir* in the science of astronomy has charmed those competent to appreciate it, both at Palermo and here, and his social qualities have won him the esteem of all who have formed his acquaintance in Italy. It is pleasant to witness Sir William Gell's delight in meeting any scientific person, from whom he can derive knowledge on any subject. Far from being content with his own acquirements, which are various, he grasps at every opportunity of adding to his store, with all the freshness of intellect of a youth of seventeen. This unquenchable thirst for knowledge preserves his mind in all its pristine freshness, and precludes the possibility of his experiencing the *taedium vitae* to which most people of his age are subject. He was much gratified by the conversation of Mr. Herschel, and enquired with interest into the recent discoveries and improvements in the formation of astronomical instruments. Gell brought us some extremely interesting letters from his enterprising and learned friend, Mr. Wilkinson,[2] the Egyptian traveller, to whom he is much attached.

An American fleet has arrived in the bay, and we went yesterday on board to see the ship of the commodore, Crichton. Nothing could exceed the good order and cleanliness of the vessel, nor the elegance of the cabin of the commodore. The sailors are fine-looking men, and the commodore and his officers are exceedingly gentlemanly, well informed, and intelligent. We were received with great politeness, refreshments were served in the cabin, and the band, a very good one, played several national

[1] Sir John Frederick William Herschel (1792-1871). Created a Baronet in 1838.

[2] Sir John Gardner Wilkinson (1797–1875). Explorer and Egyptologist. Went to Italy for his health in 1820 and was knighted in 1839.

airs. There is a library in each ship, from which the crew are supplied with books, each man giving a receipt for the book lent to him; and great is the demand for them. The collections are chiefly composed of voyages, biography, and history; and so great is the thirst for knowledge among the crew, that the volumes are seldom allowed to remain on the shelves. It was very gratifying to witness the rapid march of intellect evinced by all that we beheld on board the American ship; and prejudiced and unjust, indeed, must those be who, after seeing its details and *ensemble*, could deny that our trans-atlantic brethren have made a wonderful progress as a nation. A Mr. Livingstone, a passenger in the commodore's ship, is an excellent specimen of an American; being well bred, and thoroughly well informed.

We have made a very pleasant expedition to the Island of Caprea [Capri], where we staid three days. Messrs. Strangways, H. Bailie, and Millingen accompanied us, and with our own inmates, made a large party. As there is no inn at Caprea, we sent our courier, a day or two before us, to arrange for our reception; which he effected, by taking three small houses, which, by whitewashing, and thoroughly cleaning, were rendered very tolerable abodes. The *Bolivar* was freighted with provisions; and on the island we found fish that might have satisfied even the fastidious palate of a Lucullus.

The views from Caprea are charming. On one side, Naples is seen with her cupolas, steeples, and minarets bounding the blue waters of the bay; and on the other, an extensive prospect of the sea is spread out, until it appears to mingle with the azure sky in the distant horizon. The beautiful coast of Sorrento, which is about three leagues distant, is beheld to peculiar advantage from Caprea; and the islands of Ischia, and Procida, form fine features in the picture. The balmy air is so strongly impregnated with the saline qualities of the sea, that the frame, rendered languid by the heat of Naples, soon becomes invigorated by the fresh and salubrious breezes of this island, which might be rendered a most delicious retreat during summer.

The inhabitants of Caprea, or Capri, as it is at present called, are a good-looking healthy race, and the women are peculiarly handsome. A curious instance of the *naiveté* of some of them was furnished to us, on the first evening of our arrival. Having ascended to Ana-Capri, we seated ourselves, on the route, on a platform, commanding a fine prospect, when we saw three very beautiful women approaching; dressed, for it happened to be a fête-day, in their holiday costume, which is exceedingly rich, picturesque, and becoming. We remarked their beauty, but as our observations were made in English, they could not comprehend the praise we bestowed; and in passing, smiled, and nodded to us, with that grace peculiar to Italian women. They descended a few of the five hundred steps of the declivity that separates Ana-Capri from Capri; when they quickly returned, and running up to us, alternately clasped me in their arms, with every demonstration of affection; apologising for the liberty they had taken, by declaring that an irresistible sentiment, a *"simpatia"* urged them to its commission. Our party were exceedingly amused by this burst of natural feeling; and as the women were perfectly clean, I joined in the laugh it excited, with more mirth than I should have experienced if my embracers had been less free from symptoms of personal neglect.

The ascent to Ana- Capri is very fatiguing, but the view, and fresh breezes, repay the trouble of mounting above five hundred steps. We made the circuit of the island on mules; and on the eastern promontory the site of the palace of Tiberius was pointed out to us, which was an admirable position. We then rode to the *piscina*, and explored the ruins, among which are the remains of a theatre and baths. In the latter place we found several small fragments of rich and rare marbles; and I picked up a piece of false opal, which, except with experienced judges, might pass for the real stone. The ancients had arrived at an extraordinary degree of perfection in the imitation of gems; for I have seen several in Italy, that, until minutely examined, I believed to be genuine. They excelled, also, in the fusion of different compositions with glass, an art now nearly lost; and at Rome, specimens were shown me of great beauty.

The day after our arrival at Capri, the handsome peasant women, whom we encountered on the platform at Ana-Capri, brought large bouquets of flowers for my acceptance; and pressed me, with a graceful warmth, to make their island my residence. Among the many inducements held out, were the health I should enjoy, – no one, as they asserted, ever being ill at Capri; the long duration of youth, and its attractions, (no trivial inducement to a woman;) and though last, not least, the empire that would be gladly accorded to one, who would suffer herself to be loved by the inhabitants. In short, they said I should be their queen; a distinction which they declared had never before been offered to any other person – and all this homage and affection, was the effect of *simpatia*. In our colder country this feeling could not be understood; for, though we also experience the magnetic attraction which some countenances possess, and are as strongly repulsed by others, which nevertheless may not be positively disagreeable, yet as the usages of society prevent us from yielding to our impulses, we can hardly imagine how wholly these simple people abandon themselves to theirs. Good looks have, I believe, nothing to do in exciting this same *simpatia*; it is some benevolent expression of countenance that gives birth to it. The superstitious dread of an evil eye, so generally felt in Italy, originates, I imagine, in the disagreeable impression produced on this sensitive people by an ill-natured, or repulsive aspect; for I have seen the peasants turn abruptly away from a severe, or stern visage, although the features were faultless.

The ex-Empress of France, Marie-Louise,[1] has arrived on a visit to the King of Naples. I saw her yesterday, and a less interesting-looking woman I have seldom beheld. Her face must always have been plain, for neither the features nor expression are such as constitute good looks. The first are truly Austrian; the nose rather flat, the forehead anything but intellectual, the eyes a very light blue, and of an unmeaning character, and the mouth defective. Her figure is no longer round and well formed, as it is said to have been; and there is neither elegance nor dignity in her air or manner. She was attended by the Count de Nieperg,[2] her avowed chamberlain; and, as most persons assert, her not avowed husband. He is a gentleman-like looking man; and though wanting an eye, his physiognomy is not disagreeable. Now that I have seen Marie-Louise, I am not surprised at her conduct on the fall of Napoleon: the weakness and indecision of her character are visible in a countenance, which might serve as an illustration to Lavater's system, so indicative is it of imbecility. Marie-Louise had a great role to enact in the drama of life, had she only had spirit and heart enough to have filled it. Her devotion to Napoleon in his fallen fortunes, would have been as honourable to her character as soothing to his feelings; and was the more

[1] Marie-Louise (1791–1847) d. of Francis I, Emperor of Austria who m. Napoleon I as his 2nd wife in 1810.

[2] General Count Adam Albert Neipperg (1772–1829) who m. morganatically, the Empress Marie–Louise, then Duchess of Parma, in 1820.

called for, as it would have justified the subserviency and show of affection evinced towards him, while he ruled the destinies of France. How widely different has been the conduct of the Princess Catherine of Wirtemburg [Württemberg] towards her husband the ex-King of Westphalia, brother of Napoleon.[1] She nobly resisted every endeavour to induce her to renounce her husband, when driven from the throne which she shared. It was her duty, she said, never to forsake him to whom she had pledged her vows at the altar; and his misfortunes only served to render this duty still more imperative. How forcibly must the contrast afforded by the conduct of these two princesses, have struck Napoleon, when pining in exile; and how must it have aggravated the bitterness of his feelings, at this unnatural desertion, when, chained on a rock, Prometheus-like, he fed on his own heart!

Last night, I witnessed one of the most beautiful scenes imaginable. It was a sort of fête offered to Marie-Louise, by the King of Naples, and took place on the water. Never was there a more propitious night for such a festival, for not a breeze ruffled the calm bosom of the beautiful bay, which resembled a vast lake, reflecting on its glassy surface the bright sky above, which was glittering with innumerable stars. Naples, with its white colonnades, seen amidst the dark foliage of its terraced gardens, rose like an amphitheatre from the sea; and the lights streaming from the buildings on the water, seemed like columns of gold. The Castle of St. Elmo crowned the centre of the picture; Vesuvius, like a sleeping giant in grim repose, stood on the right, flanked by Mount St. Angelo, and the coast of Sorrento fading into distance; and on the left, the vine-crowned height of the Vomero, with its palaces and villas, glancing forth from the groves that surround them, was crowned by the Mount Camaldoli, with its convent spires pointing to the sky. A rich stream of music announced the coming of the royal pageant; and proceeded from a gilded barge, to which countless lamps were attached, giving it, when seen at a distance, the appearance of a vast shell of topaz, floating on a sea of sapphire. It was filled with musicians, attired in the most glittering liveries; and every stroke of the oars kept time to the music, and sent forth a silvery light from the water which they

[1] Jerome Bonaparte (1784–1860). Marshall and Kg. of Westphalia 1807–13.

rippled. This illuminated and gilded barge was followed by another, adorned by a silken canopy, from which hung curtains of the richest texture, partly drawn back to admit the balmy air. Cleopatra, when she sailed down the Cydnus, boasted not a more beautiful vessel; and as it glided over the sea, it seemed excited into motion by the music that preceded it, so perfectly did it keep time to the delicious sounds, leaving behind it a silvery track like the memory of happiness. The king himself steered the vessel; his tall and slight figure gently curved, and his snowy locks falling over ruddy cheeks, show that age has bent but not broken him. He looked simple, though he appears like one born to command; a hoary Neptune, steering over his native element: all eyes were fixed on him; but his, steadily followed the glittering barge that preceded him. Marie-Louise was the only person in the king's boat; she was richly dressed, and seemed pleased with the pageant. Innumerable vessels, filled with the lords and ladies of the court followed, but intruded not on the privacy of the regal bark, which glided before us like some gay vision or dream.

Yesterday, we went on board the *Revenge*, commanded by Admiral Sir Harry Neale.[1] It is a magnificent ship; and the admiral is the very *beau idéal* of a British flag-officer. Handsome, dignified and amiable, no wonder that he is so beloved by his crew, and so respected and esteemed by all who know him. I could have fancied myself back in dear Old England again, while on board the *Revenge*; English faces around me on every side, and English voices ringing in my ears. How the charm of such associations are felt, when one has been long away from home! There is something to be proud of, when one sees the moving English town, floating on a foreign sea, preserving all her national customs and usages as strictly as though she were anchored in some English port; the glorious flag of her country flying in the air, and her denizens actively employed in preserving that good order which has placed the British navy above all others. I experienced this feeling, mingled with tenderness, when going over this magnificent ship: it was like finding the temple of our *Dii Penates* (sic) on the ocean.

Commodore Crichton, and four or five of his officers, dined with us yesterday; they are sensible and agreeable men: one, a

---

[1] Admiral Sir Henry Burrard Neale (1765–1840). Commander-in-Chief Mediterranean 1823–26.

Captain Deacon, has his son on board, a very fine and interesting child, eight or ten years of age. It was pleasant to see the kindness and gentleness displayed towards this boy, by the messmates of his father; it was almost feminine; but there is, I think, a peculiar benevolence in the breasts of sailors, that disposes them to protect the less strong. There is a great gravity in these American seamen, yet it is wholly distinct from dullness, and seems to be the fruit of reflection: it sits well on them, – better, in my opinion, than gaiety would; for, to men passing the principal portion of their lives exposed to the treacherous element over which they float, seriousness seems but natural. It was gratifying to me to hear the regret expressed by the Americans for Byron; he would have been pleased at this homage, rendered to him by the individuals of a nation he respected; for he was keenly sensible to kindness, and had experienced too little of it from his compatriots, not to appreciate it from others.

Among the officers of the *Revenge*, Lord B. has recognised the son of an old friend, General Wemyss.[1] He has come to stay a few days with us, and is so amiable and well-informed, that he is a great acquisition to our circle. He is daily expecting his promotion of master and commander, and will be greatly regretted when he leaves the *Revenge*. I know not why it is, that people imagine that naval officers are in general rough in their manner, and more jovial than well bred. No opinion can be more erroneous; for, out of an extensive acquaintance, I never met a naval officer that was not well bred and agreeable. Mr. Wemyss, who has been at sea since he was ten years old, possesses all the high breeding and gentleness, that people think appertain peculiarly to those accustomed to pass the greater portion of their time in the most refined female society. He draws remarkably well, is fond of music, and has an extensive knowledge of literature; and is nevertheless, I am told, considered one of the best officers in the service; a proof that nautical skill is not incompatible with accomplishments and refinement.

I have become so accustomed to see my kind and excellent friends, Sirs Wm. Drummond and Gell, continually, that the loss of their society will be felt as a severe privation, whenever I sustain it. Drummond's is one of the most highly cultivated minds imaginable; and his conversation teems with instruction,

[1] General David Douglas Wemyss (1760–1839).

so happily conveyed, as to impress itself deeply on the memory. I count it one of the greatest advantages of my *séjour* at Naples, to have enjoyed so much of the society of this remarkable man; and to have inspired him with a friendship that will, I feel certain, continue while we live. I value this amity, perhaps the more, that it is bestowed but on a chosen few; while that of the good-natured Gell is accorded to all who seek it. An Italian lady said of Gell that his heart, like their churches, was open to all who chose to enter; but that Drummond's, like Paradise, was difficult to be entered, consequently one was sure to meet there but a select company.

England could not have sent out a minister to Naples, more calculated to impress its natives with a favourable opinion of the English, than Mr. Hamilton. To rare erudition, he unites a fine taste and agreeable manners; and is universally esteemed and respected. His skill, as a *virtuoso*, is worthy of being classed with that of his distinguished countryman, and, I believe, relative, Sir William Hamilton, so long minister here.

We have spent four or five days very agreeably at the island of Ischia; Mr. J. Strangways accompanied us there. It is a delightful spot, and the homeliness of its accommodations is not without its charms. We stopped to see the beautiful island of Nisida, which looks as if formed for the residence of fairies, so fresh and bright is its verdure, and so picturesque, yet *petite*, is its *ensemble*. While at Ischia, we ascended the Monte di Vico, and Monte d'Epomeo, which command the most enchanting views imaginable. A hermit resides in a cave at the summit of the latter; and did the honours of his rude dwelling with much urbanity and intelligence. The ascent is exceedingly abrupt; and the latter part of it we were compelled to accomplish on foot, leaving our mules behind us. From the hermitage, the island is looked down on, with its vines and figs, presenting a mass of brilliant verdure, only broken by the stone terraces that crown nearly all the flat-roofed houses; many of them surrounded with rustic trelliswork, overgrown by flowering plants, or vines. The blue and sparkling sea is spread out as if to serve as a mirror to the azure sky that canopies it; and the white sails that float on it, resemble swans gliding over some vast and tranquil lake . . .

On returning, our guide led us by a still more abrupt path than the one by which we had ascended; and the mode by which the muleteers got their mules down some of the worst parts of the route, surprised me. A few of them went below, while others forced the animal head foremost to the edge of the summit of the steep; and, holding it by the tail, to prevent it from falling, let it gradually descend, until the men beneath, who had clambered up a portion of the ascent to encounter it, were enabled to grasp it, and assist it to the bottom. The loud neighing of the mules, and the cries, exclamations, and curses of the muleteers, formed a chorus by no means harmonious; and when the feat was accomplished, the laughter in which the men indulged, as they imitated the kicking and neighing of the mules, was irresistibly comic.

The lower class of Italians in general, and the Neapolitans in particular, have a decided taste and talent for buffoonery, which breaks forth on every occasion. Innumerable examples of this propensity may be witnessed, on pausing to observe any group assembled on the quay, or in the streets. I have frequently been amused by seeing the drollery with which some of the *lazzoroni* mimic each other, when I have been waiting for our boat on the *molo*; they cannot repeat a story without giving an imitation of the persons engaged in it; and this is done in so comic a way, that few actors could do it better.

During our *séjour* at Ischia, we were much gratified by the music heard nightly in the little hamlets, as we returned from our evening rides; groups of three and four persons, with guitars, were seen seated on a terrace, or on a bench before their houses, singing Neapolitan airs, and barcaroles, in a style that would not have offended the ears of Rossini himself; while, in another quarter might be found a party dancing the merry *tarantella*, to the sound of a guitar and tambourine, to which their voices, as well as their feet, kept perfect measure. Rarely did we pass two hundred yards without meeting such groups; and when we paused to listen to their songs, or see the dancing, they invariably offered us seats, and them continued, without any embarrassment.

The fête-dress of the female inhabitants of Ischia is very picturesque and becoming, and totally unlike that of the Neapolitan women; the men wear scarlet caps, of the Phrygian shape, and are a fine-looking and hardy race. The females are much handsomer than those of Naples; and have very expressive countenances, and gentle manners. The mud, sand, and mineral baths at Ischia are considered very beneficial in rheumatic and cutaneous diseases, and are much frequented.

On our return, we stopped to see the island of Procida, which, though much inferior to Ischia, is well worthy of being visited. Here wine, bread, grapes, and figs, of the most delicious quality, were offered to us by the women; and one or two of the houses which we entered, though homely to the last degree, were so clean, that the fruit presented to us in them might be eaten without the smallest apprehension, or dread.

When passing beneath the Promontory of Misenum, we saw several flights of the flying-fish. They were small, with very bright hues, which shone radiantly, as they rose dripping from the surface of the sea, and soared to a short distance, not ascending higher than five or six feet, and then sinking into the water again. It was a very beautiful sight, and but rarely seen here.

A peculiar charm of Naples is the variety of delightful places in its environs; whither, when tired of the town, its inhabitants can repair and totally change the scene. Sorrento, whence we are but just returned, is, in my opinion, one of the most pleasant spots for a summer residence that I ever saw; and whether approached by land or water, offers the most striking and attractive scene imaginable. The view from the Promontory of Sorrento is magnificent; and the ruins scattered through the place give it additional attractions. But those fragments of antiquity, interesting as they are, had less charms for me than the spot where the gifted, but unhappy poet, Tasso, first saw the light . . .

The plain of Sorrento is divided into gardens, in which bloom the orange, pomegranate, aloe, and other trees, with various odoriferous plants, which grow with a luxuriance I never previously saw equalled. The peaches, figs, and grapes, are abundant and of a delicious flavour; and flowers that in our chilly latitudes are only to be seen in hot-houses, may here be encountered in the gardens of every peasant. Sorrento, viewed from any of the hills that overlook it, seems one mass of orange and lemon trees, with their golden fruit and snowy flowers glittering beneath the sunbeams; while the lofty stonepine, cedar, oak, and cypress, lift their heads far above them, as if to guard the rich and glowing fruit. The town of Sorrento is very picturesque. Above it, and between the houses, is the richest and brightest foliage, while its walls are bathed by a sea, blue as the sky that overhangs it. Fishermen, with their scarlet Phrygian caps, are seen conveying baskets laden with fish of the most brilliant colours; and peasants, in their fanciful costumes, are passing along bearing piles of the most tempting fruit, crowned with bouquets of odour-breathing flowers. This mixture of the fruits and flowers of earth, and the productions of the sea, brought in contact for sale, has an admirable appearance; and the mingled group of fishermen and peasants, with the surrounding scenery, would make a charming picture.

On the route to Meta, the site of a temple,[1] said to have been dedicated to Venus, was pointed out to us; near to which are two myrtle trees of such immense dimensions, that at first sight we could hardly believe them to be of the same species with the stunted myrtles of our own country. The village of Meta has a handsome church, and some of the finest olive-trees I ever saw. There is no inn at Sorrento, but excellent lodging-houses on reasonable terms may be had. An epicure will find there an abundant supply of viands of the best quality, and the poultry and veal are worthy of their reputation, being exquisitely white and delicate in their flavour. The caverns along the shore, in many of which boats are moored, and groups of fishermen may be seen reclining, look very picturesque from the sea; and are said to have furnished the models of many of the pictures of Salvator Rosa. Taken altogether, Sorrento, in my opinion, offers the most delightful residence of any place in the environs of Naples; and to those who like retirement and beautiful scenery, is preferable to it.

October 1824. – Now that the equinoctial winds have reminded us how much our beautiful residence, the Belvedere, stands in need of solid reparation for the winter, we find ourselves compelled to remove to the less fine, but infinitely more comfortable abode, the Villa Gallo, at Capo di Monte. It is with great regret, too, that we abandon this fine palace; but it is much more suited to a summer than to a winter residence. The gardens of the Villa Gallo are beautiful beyond description; but the rooms are neither sufficiently large, nor lofty, for my taste, especially after having so long occupied the fine apartments of the Belvedere. In three days we remove to our new abode, to the great regret of the good peasants who inhabit the lower part of Belvedere, and who have become as much attached to us as if we had passed all our lives

[1] There seems to be no record of a temple here, but a church was erected on the spot where the image of the Virgin is supposed to have dropped from the clouds and this event is celebrated at the *festa* of "Madonna del Lauro".

under the same roof. A more affectionate and grateful race than the Neapolitans cannot be found; judging by my own experience, a more honest one. We have now dwelt a considerable time amongst them, and have never lost the slightest article, notwithstanding that many things of value have been left exposed in the different apartments.

VILLA GALLO, November 1824. – We are now installed in our new residence, and a beautiful one it is; yet I regret the Belvedere. The royal family of Naples are, it would seem, less fastidious in their notions of comfort than we are; for I have just heard that they have taken it for two or three months in despite of its windows shaking at every breeze, and its unlined pale blue silk curtains waving at every gust. The air of Vomero is considered so salutary, that the Prince of Salerno, heir-apparent to the Neapolitan throne, who is in delicate health, has been induced to try its efficacy in preference to any of the royal palaces in the vicinity of Naples.

Several English have arrived for the winter. Among them are our last year's acquaintance, Mr. Henry Baillie, a very agreeable acquisition to our society, and the two Captains Dundas, sons of Lord Melville.[1] The two latter dined here to-day.

The *Cambrian*, commanded by Commodore Hamilton, has arrived at Naples. He is an old friend of Lord B.'s, and came to dine with us yesterday. There is something peculiarly agreeable in a well bred sailor, and nearly all that I know are so. How unlike the bluff, rude animals, half man, and half sea-monster, that we read of in some of the old novels, taking tobacco into the mouth, and pouring oaths out of it! The suavity of a naval officer possesses that gentleness which peculiarly appertains to a more than ordinary degree of manliness, and is, therefore, always acceptable and agreeable to women. Commodore Hamilton looks the personification of a Neptune. His stature is above the general height; he is robust and powerful, without losing any portion of its dignity and grace. His manner is that of a person accustomed to command, yet, though grave and dignified, it is full of benevolence. I can well imagine how much such a man might be missed from his home and hearth, and how anxiously his return must be looked for in his domestic circle. He referred to his family

[1] Henry, later 3rd Viscount Melville who d. 1876 and Robert, later 4th Viscount Melville (1803–1886).

with a sigh, and said he had no hope of seeing them for a long time to come. What sacrifices men make for their country, when they leave those so dear to them, for an indefinite period, to encounter hardships and perils of which we, enjoying all the comforts and security of land, can form but a slight idea.

More English have arrived at Naples; and among them are Mr. Henry Fox, the son of Lord Holland,[1] and Mr. J. Townshend,[2] the son of Lord Sydney. They dined here yesterday. Mr. H. Fox possesses the talent for society in an eminent degree. He is lively, intelligent, and *très-spirituel*; seizes the points of ridicule in all whom he encounters, at a glance; and draws them out with a tact that is very amusing to the lookers-on. Mr. J. Townshend is amiable, well bred, and agreeable, perfectly free from vanity, though with much that might excuse, if not justify such a weakness, being very good-looking.

The *Sybil*, Captain Pechel,[3] has arrived at Naples, and he came to dine with us yesterday, bringing with him a fine youth, the son of Lord Carlisle; and young Tollemache, a relative of Lord B[lessington]'s, both of whom are midshipmen on board his ship. We have obtained permission for them to spend a few days with us, and they seem greatly to enjoy their visit. Captain Pechel is very agreeable; full of good sense, and knowledge of the world. He has lost no occasion of gaining information; and its acquirement has not been obtained at the expense of any portion of the good-nature, and kindness of heart, for which he is so remarkable, and, for which he is so much esteemed by all his friends.

We have now been so long residents here, that we have formed not only intimacies with many, but friendships with some, of the Neapolitans. The family of the Count de Camaldoli[4] is that to which we feel the most attached; and it would be difficult, if not impossible, to encounter persons more highly gifted, and amiable, than the different members of it. They are, and deservedly, considered the most distinguished at Naples; for their men-

---

[1] Hon. Henry Edward Fox, 4th Baron Holland, b. 1802 and suc. his father in 1840.

[2] John Robert Townshend, 3rd Viscount Sidney, later Earl Sidney, (1805–1890).

[3] Rear-Admiral Sir Samuel John Brooke Pechell (1785–1849).

[4] Giuseppe Ricciardi, conte di Camaldoli, whose father Francesco, was Minister of Justice and created a count by Murat. His Villa on the Vomero was renowned for its garden – it is now a home for the Blind.

tal endowments, high cultivation, and well-known benevolence. Possessed of a large fortune, the Count de Camaldoli makes a noble use of it; for, independent of exercising a liberal and refined hospitality, he is the generous and enlightened patron of arts and science: and at his delightful abode, may always be met the most distinguished poets, painters, sculptors, and architects, as well as the most remarkable statesmen, and Neapolitan nobility. Strangers may well consider themselves fortunate, who can obtain an introduction to this charming family; in whose domestic circle, the constant practice of every virtue is united with a love and knowledge of the fine arts, rarely acquired, except by artists. The Count de Camaldoli is looked on as the man in Naples the best calculated to be prime minister; but those who witness the happiness he diffuses, and enjoys, in his home, can never wish, however advantageous it might be to his country, to see him exchange the tranquil, useful, and honourable life he now leads, for the more brilliant, but less happy career for which he is considered to be so well qualified.

The Countess Camaldoli is beloved by all who know her; and scarcely less than adored, by her husband and children, over whose happiness she watches like a presiding deity.

The two daughters of this excellent couple, are perfect musicians; and sing in a style rarely attained by musical amateurs. They draw, and paint admirably; one of them is esteemed a first-rate mathematician, and the other a good poet. Their conversation is full of general information; so unostentatiously and agreeably conveyed, that they never can be suspected of pedantry. The two sons are what might be expected, from such parents. The elder, an admirable scholar, is full of good sense, and will one day emulate the fine qualities of his father: the second, is a youth of rare genius, already the author of poems, that give the promise of no common success, when a few more years are added to his age; for he is now not more than fifteen or sixteen. Never have I witnessed, even in dear England, such devoted affection in any domestic circle, as in that of the Count de Camaldoli. For with us, though the daughters of family may be as fondly attached as are these amiable girls to their parents, the sons, from having received a public education, are apt to lose that devotion to home and its inmates, which characterise the young Riciardis; who, brought up beneath the paternal roof, have never been separated from their family. Well might the venerable archbishop of Tarentum pronounce the Ricciardis to be the model which all Italians ought to copy; and the family which he would select, as being most calculated to convey to strangers the best impression of the Neapolitan domestic character.

General Church[1] dined with us yesterday; he is full of military ardour, and has studied his profession *con amore*. He has introduced General Florestan Pepe[2] to us, who is clever, intelligent, and agreeable. Filangieri, Prince Satriano,[3] is one of the most distinguished men in Italy, not only as a soldier, but as a scholar. We made his acquaintance at the house of the good Camaldoli, and consider his society to be one of the most desirable acquisitions we have made since our arrival here. Nothing can be more delightful than the evenings passed with those with whom we are the most intimate here. Music of the very best kind, and conversation stored with information and interest, fill up the hours; while the total absence of ceremony and constraint, impart to even an extensive circle, all the freedom and charm of a family one.

The Duc[4] and Duchesse de—— dined with us yesterday. He was, formerly, ambassador from Naples at Paris, and was at Campo-Formio when Napoleon displayed so much ill-humour, relative to the treaty. He abounds in diplomatic anecdotes, which he loves to relate. The Duchesse is lively, good-natured, and good-looking; she is a descendant of the ancient and noble, Roman family of Colonna, of whom, however, I discovered in a conversation with her, she knows much less than I do. She seemed surprised when I talked of the intimacy of Petrarch with her ancestor Stephen; and still more so, when I named her charming relative Vittoria Colonna, the wife of the celebrated Duc del Vasto, and the friend of Michael Angelo; nor had she ever heard

[1] General Sir Richard Church (1784–1873). Present at Battle of Maida (1806) and was sent to defend Capri against Murat (1806). British Military Resident in Italian army against Murat and later accepted the rank of major-general in Neapolitan service. Became Governor of the two Apulian provinces of Terra di Bari and Terra di Otranto with special mission to suppress brigandage.

[2] General Florestano Pepe di Squillacè (1780–1851). Governor of Naples 1815.

[3] Carlo Filangieri, principe di Satriano and duca di Taormina (1784–1867)

[4] Marchese Marzio Mastrilli, duca di Gallo.

of her beautiful sonnets, until I spoke of them. She smiled at hearing that she had a poetess among her ancestors; when the Duc explained that the early marriage of the Duchesse, the care of her large family, and her love of music, prevented her knowing as much of past times as could be wished; to which assertion she assented with a charming *naiveté*. Accomplishments are in general more attended to in Italy, in the education of women, than is literary instruction. Most of them can charm the ear by their fine, and well-taught music, and can exhibit masterly sketches in their portfolios; but it is not often that highly cultivated minds, capable of affording delight in conversation, can be found. When they are met, however, as in the case of the ladies of the Ricciardi family, and some others, it must be admitted, that in versatility of acquirements, the women of no other country can be more admirably educated, or more formed to make rational and agreeable companions.

All the inhabitants of Naples are in a state of excitement, caused by the murder of Mr. and Mrs. Hunt;[1] which shocking event occurred close to Paestum, on their return from that place. Murder, or indeed robberies, have been so unfrequent during the last few years, that this one has surprised, nearly as much as it has shocked, the Neapolitans.

Mr. and Mrs. Hunt were both in the bloom of youth; newly married, they had set out for Italy immediately after their nuptials; little anticipating that in the beautiful land which they eagerly journeyed to see, they should so soon encounter a premature and violent death. I met them at Naples but three days previously to the fatal event: and was so struck with the beauty of this ill-fated young woman that I enquired her name; now that I hear it coupled with a horrible death, I can hardly bring myself to think that one I so lately saw full of life and health, is indeed her whose murder is the topic of every one I meet. The youth, personal attractions, and fond attachment of this young couple, have awakened a lively interest and regret in the minds of all who are acquainted with the sad tale of their deaths. They were on their return from Paestum, attended only by a man servant, who was on the box of their *calèche*, when three or four armed brigands stopped the carriage, and menaced them with death, unless they

[1] Thomas Welch Hunt of Wadenhoe. High Sheriff of Northampton in 1823 who m. Caroline, d. of Rev. C. E. Isham, Rector of Polebrook, in 1824.

immediately delivered their money and baggage. Mr. Hunt, a fine, spirited young man, was more disposed to offer resistance, than to comply with this demand; but Mrs. Hunt, greatly alarmed, entreated him to give them the bag of dollars which was in the carriage, beneath their feet. His servant remonstrated with the brigands; who, incensed at his interference, violently struck him. Mr. Hunt stooped down, whether to seize the bag of dollars, or fire-arms, is not known: the brigands thought the latter was his intention, and they instantly fired at him. Mrs. Hunt, seeing a robber take aim at her husband, threw herself between them, clasping him in her arms, and received two balls, which passed from her person to his, mortally wounding both.

The brigands fled with their booty; and some peasants hearing the shot came to the spot, and found the young couple nearly insensible, and weltering in their blood. They removed the husband into the next hut on the road, where he soon expired; and took Mrs. Hunt back to the wretched abode at Paestum, which she had so lately quitted in the enjoyment of as much happiness as falls to the lot of mortals. The melancholy intelligence soon spread, and next day reached the residence of the worthy Miss White,[1] an English maiden lady, of advanced years, who inhabits a house at La Cava, and she soon set out on horse-back, to offer her services to her unhappy countrywoman. In the meanwhile, two young officers of the *Revenge*, who had gone to see Paestum, arrived there within a short time of the fatal catastrophe, and undertook the care of Mrs. Hunt; on whom they waited with all the tenderness and delicacy that could have been expected from the gentlest of her own sex. She, poor soul! kept enquiring continually for her husband, who she was told was doing well, in a house at a short distance, but whence it would be dangerous to remove him; she then entreated to be taken to him, making light of her own wound, which was so soon to consign her to the grave. She appeared to have no sense of her own danger; and preserved a degree of cheerfulness to the last, reverting to her distant home, and those dear relatives she was never more to behold; who would, as she asserted, be so grateful to her two kind young countrymen, who nursed her as though she were their sister. The wound produced fever and delirium, during the

[1] Miss Anna Baptista White or Whyte, friend of Sir William Gell and Sir Walter Scott. She died at St. Jorio, near Portici on 28 Nov. 1833 and was buried at Naples.

paroxysms of which, she raved of her husband; congratulated herself on having saved him at the expense of her own danger; addressed the most affectionate expressions to the far distant relatives, whom she believed to be close by her bed; and sang snatches of songs in voice so harmonious, that those who heard it could hardly bring themselves to think, that it would soon be hushed for ever. She died the evening of the next day, unconscious of all that had occurred; and Miss White arrived only to see the corpse of her she would have so tenderly succoured.

The first news I heard on awaking this morning, was the decease of the King of Naples. He was found dead in his bed, by his attendants, without having suffered any previous illness; having been in perfect health last night when he retired to that chamber which he was never more to leave, but as a corpse. His death appears to have occurred while he slept; for all about him indicated that no struggle had taken place. He is much regretted, for if not a sovereign of superior mental acquirements, he was assuredly a good-natured man. I was reminded of the sentiments of the same class of individuals in Ireland, today, when I walked in the pleasure grounds, and heard the peasants comment on this event, in something like the following terms:

"Ah! Signora, how hard it is to be compelled to die, when one possessed all that could render life desirable. *Corpo di Bacco!* it is a sad affair. Now, for one of us, who only know a life of labour, and privation, it is a different thing; but for a king to be forced to leave behind him all that can delight the heart of man! Yes, it is a hard thing."

I saw the deceased Soverign, only two days ago, looking healthy and vigorous; and now – another sits in his place. His successor, and the Royal Family, have come to the palace at Capo di Monte, close to this place; and the route is filled by the carriages of the ministers of state, officers of the palace, and courtiers hurrying to worship the new king, and totally oblivious of the departed one.

Various are the reports in circulation, relative to the probable changes in the administration. The liberal party, anticipating that they will be called to hold office; and the other party calculating, and, I think, with more likelihood of their expectations being fulfilled, that they will continue in power. Innumerable are the virtues, hitherto unsuspected, but now attributed to the king [Francis I], and the errors discovered in the late. It would seem that in new sovereigns, like brides, their good qualities are lauded, and their defects overlooked; for during a long residence at Naples, I never heard so many anecdotes in favour of Francesco, as in the last two days. How long will it be before a reaction takes place, and people begin to find, that after all the good old king was an excellent monarch? For thus it ever is; sovereigns, like other public characters, seldom preserve their popularity long; for they cannot satisfy the unreasonable expectations of all parties.

The Count de Camaldoli came to dine with us yesterday. No sooner was it discovered that he had been seen on the road to Capo di Monte, than a rumour was circulated that he had been sent for by the king; and as he staid with us until twelve o'clock at night, it was asserted that they had been closeted until a late hour. On the faith of this report, half Naples believes that he will be the new premier; while he is, perhaps, the only person who neither expects nor desires the office: for he is too wise to wish to forego the happiness he at present enjoys in his domestic life, and its peaceful occupations, for the laborious, though by so many coveted, dignity of first minister. It not unfrequently occurs, as in the case of this excellent man, that those who are the most fitted to fill situations of high responsibility, are precisely those who least desire them: While men, destitute of the qualities indispensable for holding office, ardently aspire to attain, and pertinaciously cling, to its possession, in defiance of the reproaches inflicted by conscience and public opinion. The family of the Count Camaldoli would deplore any advancement, however flattering, that robbed them of any portion of the society of their good father.

General Church, who dined here yesterday, proposed to conduct me to see the remains of the late king, lying in state in the Palace at Naples; and I this day availed myself of his offer. What a changed aspect did the palace present, since I had seen it last, though but a few days before! The staircase, and suite of rooms leading to the chamber of death, were hung with black, and lighted with funeral torches. Mutes and soldiers, with their arms covered with black crape, paced silently along; and all the persons attached to the palace were clothed in deep mourning. In the middle of a large and lofty chamber, lined with black velvet, spotted with silver tears, a high platform, covered with the same material, trimmed with deep silver lace and bullion fringe, was erected. On it a catafalque, surmounted by a royal crown, was placed, composed of cloth of gold and silver, and having at the four corners large plumes of feathers. On this catafalque reposed the mortal remains of the deceased king, the head elevated on a pillow, covered with cloth of gold and silver, and the face exposed. Officers of state sat at each corner of the platform; an innumerable quantity of waxen serges of huge dimensions, in silver stands, were distributed around; and large candelabra and sconces of silver, were placed against the walls. Not a sound broke the silence of the place; the floors of the apartments being covered with black carpets, of so thick a substance that no step would be heard. There lay the face I had so lately seen in health; the white locks I had often marked floating over the ruddy cheeks, now pale and marble-like. The hand, thus motionless, a few hours ago swayed a sceptre; and at this moment it cannot chase away the insolent fly that has settled on that pallid cheek! Death, at all times a most solemn and imposing sight, never appeared to me invested with more solemnity than to-day, when I saw it surrounded with all the insignia of worldly power and grandeur, over which it waved its triumphal but sombre banner. I thought of the evening, only a few months ago, when I beheld him, who, now lay so cold and immovable on the splendid catafalque before me, steering his gilded bark over the waters, "the observed of all observers." His nod was then as a law, and on his fiat, life or death depended; yet is he now humbled to the dust, the very grandeur of the trophies that surround his earthly remains seeming but as a mockery, when contrasted with the ghastly spectacle which they are meant to honour and to dignify! And his successor will put on the crown, and dwell in the stately and gilded palaces, in which that poor pale shadow of departed greatness lived; and will feast, and rejoice, and influence, as _he_ did, the destiny of hundreds. Yet can he not avert his own! for a greater, a sterner Monarch, will in turn summon _him_ away; and those who now tremble at his power, will flock to view his inanimate form, wondering how a creature frail as themselves, should have filled their breasts with such fear and awe; forgetful that to his successors they will again transfer similar homage and idolatry.

The silver tears on the hangings, were the only ones I witnessed in the chamber of death; and it struck me that they were a happy invention for such occasions. As dead kings are rarely wept for, their disappointed subjects (and how many of them, even under the sway of the best sovereigns are to be found!) look to his successor for the fulfilment of their frustrated expectations, which the new one, in his turn, is probably destined to equally disappoint. To be flattered in life, and unmourned in death, seems to be the fate of monarchs, whatever may be their merits; and yet they are the envied of earth, by those, who looking but to the surface of things, see only power, grandeur, and wealth, and behold not the cares beneath.

A curious incident lately occurred in our immediate neighbourhood. A gentleman who has a villa near this, dreamt that a certain number would be a prize in the lottery. The morning after his dream, which was only a week previous to the drawing of the lottery, he wrote a note to his clerk to desire to buy the ticket immediately: and subsequently told many of his neighbours and acquaintances of his dream, the number, and of his purchase of the ticket. Being a very popular person, all who heard of the circumstances were anxious that his dream should be realised; and, to their great satisfaction, the number was drawn a very large prize. Forthwith, a numerous party of artisans and peasants, employed by the gentleman in question, sallied forth from Naples, with musical instruments, colours flying, and a banner gaily decorated; on which the lucky number was inscribed, and also the amount of the prize. In this manner they proceeded to the habitation of Mr. ——, and announced the joyful intelligence, which, it is needless to say, spread a general hilarity through the house. This procession was followed by several friends and acquaintances, who came to congratulate the fortunate owner of the prize. Refreshments in abundance were served out on the lawn for the peasants and artisans; and a collation in the *salle-à-manger* was offered to the friends. Sufficient wine of an inferior quality not being in the cellar, the best was copiously supplied, in the generosity occasioned by the good fortune of the host. The health of the winner of the prize was repeatedly drunk; and many suggestions relative to the disposal of a portion of the newly acquired wealth were given. The news spread, and the pleasure grounds of Mr. —— became literally filled with visitors of all classes; when, in the midst of the general rejoicings, the clerk who had been a week before deputed to purchase the ticket arrived, with a visage so rueful and woe-begone, that one glance at it announced some disagreeable news. Alas! this unlucky

wight had, in the pressure of more than ordinary business, forgotten to buy the ticket! and thought not of it until informed of its
having been drawn a prize.

The rage of disappointment of Mr. —— may be more easily
imagined than described, when he saw the wheel of fortune,
which had paused at his door, driven to that of another; who,
having heard of the dream of Mr. ——, selected the number, and
became the buyer of the ticket only the day before it was drawn.
The refreshments so liberally dispensed on this occasion had
quite exhausted the larder of the dreamer, and nearly emptied his
cellar: and thus ended the affair of the lottery.

Never were people so addicted to this species of gambling as
are the Neapolitans. All classes indulge in it, more or less, but the
lower ones give way to it with an extraordinary recklessness.
Every dream, encounter, incident, or accident, has its own particular sign and number, which may be found in a book published
for the instruction of the buyers of tickets, and of which every
house has a copy. The death of a friend, however lamented,
refers to a particular number, which the mourner forgets not to
secure, if it comes in conjunction with some fortunate sign: thus
even out of misfortunes and afflictions the Neapolitans seek to
draw some recompense. Nor does frequent disappointment
seem to correct their eagerness for the lottery. They always discover some satisfactory reason for having missed the prize; and
hope to be more fortunate the next time.

May 1825. – Went yesterday to see the Lunatic Asylum at Aversa.
This town, which is of considerable extent, owes its construction
to the Normans, and occupies the site of the ancient Atella; so
celebrated for those farces, which are said to have been the
prototypes of that species of amusement in Italy, for which the
people have not even yet lost the taste. Strange metamorphosis,
from a theatre of unlicensed merriment, to a mad-house!

Aversa seems destined to be ever the scene where unbridled
passions assert their wild empire. It was near to it, that the
unfortunate Andrew, the husband of Queen Joan the first,[1] of
Naples, lost his life, in a manner that furnished presumptive
evidence that if not chargeable with, she was at least, implicated
in the crime. When the reputation attached of old to this place is

[1] Born 1326, reigned 1431–81. m. Andrew son of Charles of Hungary.

reflected on, it may be a question for casuists to decide, whether the Oscan inhabitants of the ancient Atella, or the prisoners of the modern Aversa, were the more insane. One thing is certain, which is, that the present occupants of the place are under better government than the former, and that their folly can injure none: and this is something gained.

The attention paid to the comfort of the insane in this establishment, extends not only to their persons, but to their minds; and many are the satisfactory results with which this rational and merciful treatment have been attended.

The opulent, when afflicted with the dread malady of loss of reason, can here find the most skilful care and judicious attention to their wants, for which a moderate yearly sum is paid, while they continue in the asylum; and the poor are received gratis. The first named class occupy chambers, fitted up with the same attention to their comfort as if they were in their own homes. Hot and cold baths, an extensive library, a theatre, a concert room, an apartment appropriated to astronomical instruments, and another to experiments in electricity, galvanism, and chemistry, are comprised within the building. In short, the establishment resembles one of those arranged for the reception of inmates of cultivated minds, and refined habits; and such, many of the pensioners at Aversa have become, who entered it in a state of violent mental aberation, that gave little hope of their recovery.

So anxious are the superintendents of the *Maison de Santé* to avoid wounding the feelings of their patients, that to banish even the semblance of confinement, the iron bars that secure the windows are constructed in the form of vases filled with flowers, painted on the interior and exterior, of the bright colours of the productions of which they are made in imitation. Those who are not violent, are permitted to take their repasts together; and a strict attention, not only to cleanliness, but even to elegance of the toilette, is enjoined. Comedies are performed twice a week, and of concerts an equal number. Balls are permitted whenever a desire for dancing is manifested; and the patients are allowed to devote their mornings to any occupations most congenial to their tastes, idleness being prohibited. Tragedies are considered too exciting; but comedies are supposed to have a salutary effect on the minds of the inmates. The performers are the patients, as are also the musicians of the concerts; and I have been told by those who have witnessed the performance, that it is so good as to defy the possibility of suspecting that the actors are deranged. Of the concerts, I can speak from my own knowledge, for we were permitted to be present at one, composed of various pieces, all of which were admirably played. Many of the individuals, who entered the establishment without any knowledge of music, have subsequently evinced such a predilection for it, that when facilities for acquiring it have been afforded them, they have seldom failed in becoming skilful performers. Of this fact, several examples were given to us. The soothing effect of music on the mind, has been found advantageous in the treatment of the patients; and a desire to acquire the accomplishment is considered a favourable symptom. In the library, we found several persons occupied in reading; and more than one employed in making notes. So grave, and collected, was the aspect of each, that no observer could have imagined that their intellectual faculties had ever been deranged; much less, that they were then under the influence of insanity. On passing near the reading-desk of one, my eye glanced over the work he was perusing, and I discovered it to be a folio volume of the works of Calvin. The reader was too engrossed by his study, that it was only when we approached close to him that he became conscious of our presence. He instantly rose, took off his velvet cap, bowed politely, and smiling, made a pleasant allusion to the work, he had been reading, by pointing to his head, which was very bald; thereby indicating a quibble on the word of Calvin . . .

Having examined the portion of the establishment assigned to the upper class, we were conducted to that appropriated to the lower; and here, a different scene awaited us. All was hilarity or grief, the indications of both sentiments being boisterously displayed. Many of the patients crowded round us, requesting snuff, or coffee. Not a few questioned us with an air of anxiety, that saddened one to observe, whether we brought them intelligence from home: while others entrusted us to take charge of letters to their friends to apprise them of the ill-usage to which they were subjected . . .

I turned away saddened, from this too similar, but exaggerated representation of the vices of society, to pause at the open cell of a priest, who was prostrate before a wooden cross of his own manufacture. The crown of his head was shorn, but long locks of snowy hue fell from the sides of it, and mingled with his beard of the same venerable colour, which reached to the cord that confined his robe round the waist. His face was pale as death, and his eyes, which were raised to the cross, were filled with tears, which chased each other down his attenuated cheeks. He was not sensible that several persons were around him, and he prayed with a fervour truly edifying; the words of the prayer breathing the very soul of piety, Christian resignation, and adoration for the Diety . . .

I left not this enthusiast unmoved. The earnestness of his prayers, and his total abstraction from all worldly concerns, made a deep impression on me. His life of sanctity, in the midst of the herd of maniacs with whom he was surrounded, with, but not of them, reminded me of some pure stream gliding through a turbulent river, without mingling its clear water with the turbid waves. He is pitied but beloved by the superintendent and assistants of the asylum, and derided and insulted by the patients; but he is insensible of the compassion of the first, or the contempt of the second.

Spent a most agreeable day yesterday at the Vomera, at the delightful residence of our excellent friends, the Ricciardis, where we met many clever people of both sexes; among them was Mr. Cutlar Ferguson,[1] who has long filled a high judicial office in India, and is returning to England, after an absence of many years. He is a very superior man, converses well on all subjects, and has the ease of manner peculiar to those who have seen much of the world, and mingled in some of the most distinguished of its societies.

Leoni, the celebrated *improvisatore*, made another of the party at the Count de Camaldoli's, and surprised, as well as pleased us, by the wonderful readiness with which he recited poems; many of them so elaborately pointed, and happily turned, as to convey the impression that they had been carefully polished instead of being improvised at the instant; individuals, some of whom he had never previously seen, being the subject of them. I can well imagine that a wonderful facility in versifying may be attained by the frequent exercise of this rare gift of impromptu composition; but I am persuaded that none can reach excellence in it save those remarkable, not only for highly poetical minds, but for a quickness of apprehension, and readiness of wit seldom accorded even

[1] Rt. Hon. Ronald Cutlar Ferguson, M.P. Judge Advocate General and Privy Councillor. Died at Paris in 1839.

to poets. This art, if art that may be named, which depends so much, if not entirely, on a peculiar attribute of genius, may well be called a lightning of the mind; for so vivid are the flashes of poetry which escape, as it were, from the improvisators, when in the heat of inspiration, that I can compare them with nothing but those gleams of lightning, that in summer follow each other so rapidly in hot climates. That this gift is singularly rare, is proved by the comparatively few examples of it seen even in Italy, for I cannot count mere ready rhymists improvisatores; and the solitary one in England, Mr. Theodore Hook, whose achievements in it are, I have often been told, truly surprising. In Italy, the improvisatore is encouraged, if not inspired, by the vivacity with which his points are seized, and the enthusiasm with which they are applauded; the mercurial temperaments and lively imaginations of his compatriots enabling them to appreciate every lucky hit, and applaud every poetical image. The enthusiasm he excites, animates the improvisators to still higher flights of fancy; until his eyes gleam, and his cheeks glow, as he pours out a stream of verse which, if not of profound depth, is at least bright and sparkling to the last. The exhibition reminded me of what one imagines of a Pythoness on the Tripod, at the moment of inspiration: but a consciousness of the labour and difficulty of the performance, together with the exhaustion, mental and bodily, which it must produce, detracted from my enjoyment of it. I was painfully anxious lest the Signor Leoni should break down in any of his rhymes, or fail in any of his tropes or metaphors; and so mar an achievement, in the perfect success of which, not only his *amour propre*, but his fame, might have been compromised. But my fears were groundless; he accomplished his various tasks without a single fault in the performance, and sat down amid the enthusiastic plaudits of his delighted auditors. Having been asked to give a subject to Signor Leoni, I named the death of Lord Byron. The following is the sonnet which he instantly improvised; and which a friend present, endowed with the pen of a ready writer, committed to paper as the lines were uttered. [This Poem in Italian, is not printed in this edition.]

August 1825. – Mr. Henry Fox, the son of Lord Holland, has been our inmate for some days. He is a most agreeable companion, lively, playful, and abounding in anecdote, with just enough of what the French term *malice*, to render his remarks very piquant, and just sufficient good-nature to prevent their being too satirical. The French term, *malice*, must not be taken in the sense of the broader and stronger one of the word malice, in our language. The French phrase means simply a roguishness or slyness, that induces a person to play tricks, and draw out, and exhibit the follies of his acquaintance, for the sake of exciting a laugh, without being impelled by any desire of injuring them. Henry Fox gives such admirable imitations of the peculiarities of his absent acquaintances, that those present are infinitely amused, forgetting that they in turn will furnish subjects for the talent they are now admiring. Henry Fox is just such a forced plant, as might be expected from the hot-bed culture of Holland House; where wit and talent are deemed of such importance, that more solid qualities are, sometimes, if not sacrificed to their growth, at least overlooked in the search for them. Accustomed from infancy to see all around him contributing to the amusement of the circle they compose, by a brilliant persiflage, a witty version of the *on dits* of the day, epigrammatical sallies, which though pungent, never violate *les bienséances de société*, and remarks on the literature of the day, full of point and tact, it cannot be wondered at, that he has become what he is – a most agreeable companion. As, however, he possesses no inconsiderable portion of the sweet temper and gaiety of spirits of his father, he may yet attain the more worthy distinction of becoming an estimable man.

Sir William Gell dined with us yesterday; always cheerful, though suffering under a malady that leaves him but few intervals free from acute pain. No wonder that he is so universally beloved; for independent of his social qualities, his readiness to oblige, and general philanthropy, must secure him the good-will of all who know him, and the affection of those who are favoured with his friendship. Gell can be irresistibly comic too, when so disposed; and makes one laugh for successive hours by his drollery. Perhaps, in the middle of some story, related with all the spirit and broad humour in which he abounds, a violent twinge of the gout compels a pause; when he, with tears in his eyes extracted by pain, yet with a half smile, exclaims, "Pray good Mr. Gout, take pity upon me, and let me pass one hour unmolested by your attacks. Only consider how long and patiently I have borne them; and do not wreak your vengeance on this poor, worn-out, crazy body of mine. Go to —— or ——, they will pamper you luxuriously, and saturate your spirit with brimming bumpers, while with me you will be starved outright, and chilled with the simple beverages, in which 'water from the spring' forms the principal ingredient."

On the cessation of pain, he resumes the thread of his story with all the comicality of its commencement; and those who listen, feel surprised, that he, whose drollery has so much amused them, should, though deprived of the powers of locomotion, and a prey to such frequent assaults of acute pain, have the cheerfulness, nay more, the gaiety of heart, thus to enliven and charm society.

Sir William Gell has introduced to us Mr. Richard Westmacott,[1] a young sculptor, who has been studying at Rome, and who has executed some very charming works since his residence there. He is the son of Mr. Westmacott, who has attained such a deserved reputation in London; and is a person of a highly-cultivated mind, and gentlemanly manners. Lord Dudley is one of his most zealous patrons, and spoke to us very warmly in his praise, all of which is justified by the merits of his protégé. Gell has also brought us Mr. Uwins,[2] an artist, whose works are greatly admired here; and whose society is justly deemed an acquisition, from his information and amiability. Mr. Uwins has made some very clever pictures and has given the happiest delineations of the glowing scenery and picturesque inhabitants, both of whom he has studied with all the *gusto* of a painter, who feels the beauty of his art, and is determined to attain in it the highest excellence.

November 1825. – I yesterday witnessed an exhibition of an extraordinary nature, one to be seen only in a country like this, where superstition mingles in even the most sacred and solemn things. A community is formed at Naples, each member of which, during his life, subscribes an annual sum, in order that, after death, his remains should be deposited in one of certain vaults, the earth conveyed into which has the peculiar quality of preventing decomposition, and of preserving bodies as if dried by some chemical process. But the preservation of what intended to decay, is not the only object of this institution, nor the only mode

---

[1] Sir Richard Westmacott (1775–1856). Sculptor. Knighted 1837.

[2] Thomas Uwins, R.A. (1782–1857). Painter – was in Italy 1824–31 and was Keeper of the National Gallery in 1847. See *Preface*, p. 13.

of applying its funds. The exposure, on a certain day of each year, of the frail wreck of mortality thus strangely rescued from corruption, attired in the habiliments worn by the deceased when living, is secured by the subscription; the number of annual exhibitions being dependent on the amount of the sums received. Can anything more preposterous be imagined? – nothing, I am quite sure, more disgusting can be beheld. Three or four subterraneous chapels, in the Church of Santa Chiara, divided only by partitions, are dedicated to this extraordinary exhibition, which presents one of the most ghastly scenes ever disclosed. All the sublimity of death disappears, when the poor remains of his victims are thus exposed; and instead of an appalling sight, they offer only so grotesque a one, that it is difficult to believe that the figures before one ever were instinct with life; or that they are not images formed of brown paper, or russia leather, dressed up to imitate humanity.

The subterraneous chapels are guarded by soldiers. The altars are arranged in the usual style of those in Catholic chapels; innumerable torches illuminate the place; and an abundance of flowers and religious emblems decorate it. Ranged around the walls, stand the deceased unhappily disinterred for the occasion; and clothed in dresses so little suited to their present appearance, that they render death still more hideous. Their bodies are supported round the waist by cords, concealed beneath the outward dress; but this partial support, while it precludes the corse from falling to the earth, does not prevent its assuming the most grotesque attitudes. Old and young, male and female, are here brought in juxta-position. The octogenarian, with his white locks still flowing from his temples, stands next a boy of six years old, whose ringlets have been curled for the occasion; and whose embroidered shirt-collar, and jacket with well-polished buttons, indicate the pains bestowed on his toilette. Those ringlets twine round a face resembling nothing human, a sort of mask of discoloured leather, with fallen jaws and distended lips; and the embroidered collar leaves disclosed the shrunken dark brown chest, once fair and full, where, perhaps, a fond mother's lips often were impressed; but which now looks fearful, contrasted with the snowy texture of this bit of finery. This faded image of what was once a fair child, has tied to its skeleton fingers a top, probably the last gift of affection; the hand, fallen on one side, leans towards the next disinterred corpse, whose head also, no longer capable of maintaining a perpendicular position, is turned, as if to ogle a female figure, whose ghastly and withered brow wreathed with roses, looks still more fearful from the contrast with their bright hue. Here the mature matron, her once voluminous person reduced to a sylph-like slightness, stands enveloped in the ample folds of the gaudy garb, she wore in life. The youthful wife is attired in the delicate tinted drapery put on in happy days to charm a husband's eye; the virgin wears the robe of pure white, leaving only her throat bare: and the young men are clothed in the holiday suits of which they were vain in life; some with riding-whips, and others with canes attached to their bony hands. A figure I shall never forget, was that of a young woman, who died on the day of her wedding. Robed in her bridal vest, with the chaplet of orange flowers still twined round her head, her hair fell in masses over her face and shadowy form, half veiling the discoloured hue of the visage and neck, and sweeping over her, as if to conceal the fearful triumph of death over beauty.

Each figure had a large card placed on the wall above the places they occupied; on which was inscribed the names, date of their ages, and death, with some affectionate epigraph, written by surviving friends. It would be impossible to convey the impression produced by this scene; the glare of the torches falling on the hideous faces of the dead, who seemed to grin, as if in derision of the living, who were passing and repassing in groups around them. Not a single face among the ghastly crew presented the solemn countenance we behold in the departed, during the first days of death; a countenance more touching and eloquent than life ever possessed: no, here every face, owing to the work of time, wore a grin that was appalling; and which, combined with the postures into which the bodies had fallen, presented a mixture of the horrible and the grotesque, never to be forgotten. Around several of the defunct, knelt friends, to whom in life they were dear, offering up prayers for the repose of their souls: while groups of persons, attracted merely by curiosity, sauntered through this motley assemblage of the deceased, pausing to comment on the appearance they presented . . .

I turned from this ghastly masquerade, nearly overcome by the mingled vapours of the frankincense and the torches; and by the horrors of an exhibition in which the most solemn objects were exposed to the profane gaze of crowds to be made a mockery and a jest, instead of being left to the repose of the tomb.

The Duc de Fitzjames[1] dined with us yesterday. Report says that he is come to Naples to negotiate a marriage between his aged sovereign, Charles X, and the pretty and piquante princess Christine of Naples. Probably, like the generality of reports, this one is without foundation; the ages of the parties are too disproportioned to admit of such chance of the alliance proving a happy one: nevertheless, Christine is precisely the sort of person to turn the heads of the Parisians; being elegant, graceful, and *toujours bien mise*, with a *tournure* as distinguée as even Parisians could desire

The Duc de Fitzjames is a very sensible and intelligent man, with all the knowledge of the new school, and all the high breeding of the old. There is a manly frankness in his manner and bearing, not often to be met with in those who have lived much in courts; and yet it does not deteriorate from the polish and politeness said to appertain to them: I say said, because I have seen courtiers commit as great solecisms in politeness as could be witnessed in the most uneducated.

December 1825. – Dined yesterday at the dear good Archbishop of Tarentum's, where I met *Son Altesse Royale*, the Prince Gustave of Mecklenburg Schwerin, the Duchesse de Plaisance[2] and her daughter; a German Countess with an unpronounceable name which I forget; General Count Howguitz,[3] who at present commands the Austrian troops here; the Russian Count Beckendoff, brother to the Countess Lieven, Ambassadress from Russia to our court; Sir William Gell, some Neapolitans; and, though last, not least, Casimir de la Vigne[4] the poet, and his brother.

[1] Descendant of James Fitz-James, Duke of Berwick who was a natural son of James, Duke of York (James II) by Arabella Churchill. Grandson of the then Duke of Berwick, Maddan refers to him as "this antique remnant of the ancient aristocracy of France." *op. cit.*, vol i, p. 403.

[2] Sophie de Marbois, the eccentric duchesse de Plaisance (1785–1854) who lived the latter part of her life in Athens. She began the construction of a summer palace in Gothic style on the slopes of Pendeli which was left half-finished and has only recently been completed by the Greek Royal Family. Her house at Athens is now the Byzantine Museum.

[3] Feldmarschall-Leutnant Eugen Wilhelm, Count of Haugwitz, (1752–1831). Prussian statesman. Lived in Italy after 1820.

[4] Jean François Casimir Delavigne (1793–1843). Dramatist, Satirist and Lyrist.

Son Altesse Royale is an unaffected, good-natured, well-informed, and well bred man. He is nephew to Queen Charlotte; and consequently, first-cousin to our King. Perhaps it is this relationship that renders him so remarkably polite and civil to the English; but whatever may be the cause, the effect is visible. Count Beckendoff is a very distinguished man; exceedingly good-looking, with *l'air noble*, mild and polished in manner, sensible and intelligent in conversation. He is an excellent specimen of the Russian aristocracy. Casimir de la Vigne has a *spirituelle* countenance, and very agreeable manners. There seems to exist between him and his brother a degree of fraternal affection, seldom witnessed. They are, I am told, inseparable, and are united by the bonds of sympathy as closely as by those of nature. There is a simplicity and modesty in the manners of both the brothers, that is very attractive, because it is evidently unaffected; and they are general favourites wherever they go.

The dinner was a pleasant one, which cannot often be said of dinners where the guests are composed of persons belonging to so many different countries; and who, consequently, can have but few sentiments in common. But I attribute its agreeability to the benign influence of the venerable and amiable host, whose urbanity smooths the asperities of national prejudices, and whose tact leads the conversation to subjects of general interest.

The Russian fashion of arranging the dinner table is universally adopted by the Neapolitans. A plateau and épergne occupy the centre, as with us; and the dessert, mixed with vases of flowers, occupies the places of the dishes, which in England are set on the festive board, but which here are placed on the buffet; and are carved and handed round by the servants. This mode, though it prolongs the time of dinner, is, in my opinion, a great improvement; for the economy of the table is undisturbed, and the eye is gratified by the sight of flowers and fruit, instead of contemplating the fragments of *entrées* and *relevés*; the olfactory organs too, are regaled by sweet scents, in place of mingled effluvia of fish, flesh, and fowl. Another advantage should also be named, a lady's sleeves are not crushed, nor her hair deranged, by a servant changing dishes over her shoulder.

Some of the Neapolitan dishes are excellent; and the native cooks are by no means deficient in the gastronomic *savoir-faire*. I observed that the Neapolitans, like the French, taste of all dishes, however numerous they may be, that are served at table; and that no one, except an invalid, limits his dinner to one or two. They do not eat more than English people do, but they require a greater variety. Yet, notwithstanding this indulgence in epicurism, foreigners suffer less from *"le remords de l'estomac,"* as Grimod de la Reynière delicately termed indigestion, than do the English, who confine themselves to fewer and more simple viands. I suspect that our plain roast and boiled is too nutritious for persons not taking much exercise; and that the made dishes of the French and Italians, from the meats of which the succulent juices have been nearly quite extracted by the process of cooking, are less likely to induce dyspepsia. Perhaps it is not epicurism alone that tempts foreigners to eat of all the dishes handed round; it may be politeness which prompts them not to reject what a neighbour, seated at each side, accepts; for it certainly is *gauche* to see, as I repeatedly do, at grand dinners, some fastidious English guests declining every entrée offered them, with a rueful shake of the head, and a *"non merci,"* waiting until the *roti* is carved.

The Italian confectionary and ices are far superior to those of the French and English; and their variety is infinite.

January 1826. – Filangieri (prince Satriano), the Duc Rocco Romano, the Count and Countess de Camaldoli, their accomplished daughters, and Piazzi, dined with us yesterday. The latter talked to me of Mr. Herschel; of whose acquirements he spoke in terms of warm commendation. Referring to the knowledge of Sir William Herschel and his son, he observed, "if they with their murky atmosphere and nebulous skies judge so accurately as they do, what precision ought <u>we</u> not to arrive at, with our transparent one, and cloudless heavens, where with the naked eye we can better discover the stars, than they can with a powerful glass. Your countrymen are unequalled, for their perseverance, industry, unsophisticated good sense, and total freedom from charlatanism. They have arrived near the summit of the hill of astronomical science, while we, alas! have remained at its base; though the eminence has been partly concealed from them by clouds and dense fogs, and we have had it before us, but unfortunately, like the glaciers, though exposed to view, nearly inaccessible. But you have, in your admirable constitution," continued Piazzi, "a moral sun, that can dispel the most dense clouds and fogs. Ignorance and superstition have dissolved before its influence; and with such a blessing, who would complain of the rarity of the visits of that sun, which shines so brightly on us, but alas, finds us in a state of comparative moral darkness."

Some one having, addressed Filangieri, by his title of Prince Satriano, Piazzi said, "I lose patience when I hear that new title, and wonder how he who bears it, so noble, and distinguished as he is, and so justly proud of the name bequeathed to him by his illustrious father, could sink it in any title, however elevated. Filangieri is a name which every Italian is, or should be proud of. Ancient, and noble, the family can be traced to the times when it rendered such assistance to the brave Normans, but it is still more ennobled by the father[1] of that distinguished man before us, whose works, and whose life were equally calculated to serve and reflect honour on his country."

It is pleasant to observe the enthusiasm with which the Neapolitans refer to those who have conferred distinction on their native land, nor are they less proud of the distinguished dead, than of the meritorious living, witness their admiration and affection for the Count de Camaldoli, Piazzi, Filangieri, and Rocco Romano.

The works of Filangieri, the father of the Prince Satriano, are – *Le reflessioni politiche sull' ultima legge sovrano riguardante l'amministrazione della giustizia*, and *Scienza della legislazione*: works, which acquired for their author a reputation as brilliant as durable. The mother of the Prince Satriano was one of the most remarkable women of her time. Highly educated, and devoted to her domestic duties, she was the friend and companion of her husband, in whose fame she gloried, and whose labours she cheered. It is not therefore to be wondered at, that the son of such estimable parents should be a superior man; brave in the field, wise in the council, and urbane and pleasant in society, to which his various accomplishments contribute so many attractions.

A most agreeable dinner, yesterday, at home. I like Casimir de la Vigne very much; there is a *naiveté* about him that is peculiarly attractive. Not a single symptom of vanity or affectation can be detected in his manner, and his conversation is fraught with interest. I do not wonder that he is a general favourite; the strong affection visible in his brother towards him, predisposes one to believe him as amiable as he is clever; and the warmth with which it is repaid, is a proof how well it is merited. This fraternal

[1] Gaetano Filangieri.

sentiment is not displayed, or paraded, as I have sometimes seen it in others; but is honest and true.

Few poets are, I should think, more happy than Casimir de la Vigne; indeed, judging from what I have seen of him, he seems to have escaped the moody habits and morbid sensitiveness peculiar to that irritable tribe. His is a healthy mind, satisfied with, but not overrating self, and well disposed towards all the world: he is content with the success his writings have obtained; and is more anxious to please, than astonish his readers. The Neapolitans like him exceedingly, and fête him very much; and he appears touched by their esteem, which is evinced in a manner that can leave no doubt of its sincerity. He is not made a lion of, as he would be in London, where every celebrity, no matter of what kind, is followed and stared at, until eclipsed by some new candidate for fame; but he is received with cordiality, and I might add, with affection, which cannot fail to gratify him. We are to meet him at dinner at the Count de Camaldoli's to-morrow, where all the literary people at present in Naples, are to assemble.

Casimir de la Vigne came to see me to-day, and delighted me by reciting his unpublished "columbus". It is a charming poem, and will add to his fame. He recited it admirably; and his countenance so forcibly expressed the sentiments his lips pronounced, that the verses received an additional charm. His recitation is not theatrical, yet it is very striking; and from its truth and feeling, reminded me of Moore's singing. Nothing, after all, is so calculated to create sympathy as the words being <u>truly</u> <u>felt</u> by those who repeat them, and not pronounced in a declamatory style that denotes the speaker to be more occupied with the manner, than the matter.

Colonel Hugh Bailie dined here yesterday, and met some agreeable Neapolitans, with whom he seemed pleased; among these were the handsome Madame Nicola, and her father, and the Comte Francesco Putoe.[1] I never heard a finer voice than Madame Nicola's; round, sweet, melodious, and powerful, full of passion and sentiment; the phrase used by a French connisseur, relative to the voice of a celebrated singer, might well be applied to hers, "*c'est pleine de larmes.*" Who that has drunk in the

[1] ? Conte Francesco Proto, later duca di Maddaloni – a witty versifier and epigrammatist.

dulcet notes of amateur singers in Italy, could ever listen with patience to the performances of a similar class in England? Here, the very soul of music is breathed; there, the grosser part only is expressed; here, people sing to please; there, to surprise; and it must be admitted that they generally succeed. Here, singers make you feel, because they feel what they sing; while in England, vocalists think only of the effect to be produced on others, and miss attaining their object by allowing it to be evident; in fact, they no more feel what they sing, than a musical instrument does the sound it conveys.

Music, here, may be considered as a soothing system; but English music is a positive irritation to the nerves of sensitive people.

February 1826. – As the time approaches for quitting Naples, my regret increases. A residence of nearly three years has attached me to the country and the people by ties that cannot be rent asunder without pain; and though the poet talks of "dragging at each remove a lengthening chain," memory offers no consolation for the absence of dear friends left behind, in a land that is not our land, and where we can hardly hope to come again. Some of those friends, too, are so near the goal of life, – or, should I not say, so near heaven? – that we cannot look forward to meeting them again on earth. The dear and venerable Archbishop of Tarentum, the good Piazzi! Sad thoughts recur to my mind each time I see them, now that the period for our parting is fixed, and their consciousness that our departure will be eternal, increases my despondency. The dear and amiable Ricciardis talked of travelling in France and England, so I anticipate our meeting there: but even should they not leave Italy, they are young enough not to preclude the hope, if not the certainty, of finding them in Italy once more, should I, as I trust, return; for I cannot bring myself to think that I am leaving Italy for ever.

Two agreeable English travellers, made their appearance here yesterday, with letters of introduction; Mr. Bootle Wilbraham, jun.,[1] and his cousin of the same name. Well-informed, and intelligent, they came to Italy with minds prepared for what they were to see; hence, they have neither been surprised, nor disap-

[1] ? Son of Edward Bootle-Wilbraham, created Baron Skelmersdale in 1828.

pointed, as too often happens to persons who have not previously turned their thoughts to this country. It really is gratifying to a patriotic heart, to observe the superiority of the present
generation of young Englishmen. Education, and good sense,
joined to their natural result, good manners, seem to appertain to
them all, with very few exceptions; and their bearing and conduct
are well calculated to command the respect of the foreigners
whose countries they visit. To be sure, I have met here some
young men, and of ancient descent too, who displayed a degree
of ignorance, not a little surprising, in the nineteenth century.
One, on seeing a small lachrymatory on my table, asked what it
was? A person present answered it was *a lachrymatoire.* "*A lac-
rymatoire,*" resumed the questioner, "surely it is too small to hold
enough cream, even for one cup of tea." Another seeing a small
bronze statue of Voltaire on a console, on which were placed
some antique lamps and vases, asked whether the latter were
really antique? Being assured in the affirmative, he took up the
statue of Voltaire, and observed, "Oh! for this, no one could
question its antiquity; one has only to look at it, to ascertain that it
must be an antique, the fellow looks so old."

But the ignorance of a third compatriot is even more amusing;
for living in a street at Rome, near the corner of which the filthy
scrapings of the streets were permitted to be deposited, he
believed the inscription expressive of this fact to be the name of
the street, and dated his letters, *Strada immondezza;* to the no small
amusement of his correspondents.

Yet, these are but three solitary examples of ignorance; and I
have met innumerable young Englishmen, since I have been on
the Continent, who might be cited for their general information
and abilities. Should this journal ever see the light, my three
ignorant acquaintances, will if they ever read it, acknowledge the
exactitude of my statement, and thank me for not naming them.
In detailing the ignorance of these my compatriots, I ought not to
omit noticing that of a Neapolitan; who inquired of a newly
arrived Englishman, whether he had come from England by sea,
or land.

Yes, leave-taking is a painful thing; and I felt it so yesterday,
most deeply, when I bade adieu to some very dear friends at
Naples. Their regret, justified mine; and I was not ashamed of the
tears that bathed my cheeks, when I saw theirs flowing. During
the last week, which we passed at the hotel of the *Grande Bre-*

tagne, our *salon* has been filled every evening with friends anxious to spend the last evenings of our *séjour* here, with us; and innumerable are the gifts presented to us as *gages d'amité*, endeared by our regard for the donors.

I have seldom been more affected than the day before my departure from *Naples*; when I went to bid farewell, to the dear and venerable Archbishop of Tarentum. I found him in tears, surrounded by three or four friends, who were offering him consolation. No sooner had his major-domo announced us, than this amiable prelate rose from his seat, and advanced to embrace us as rapidly as his trembling limbs would permit; exclaiming, "Ah! you see my dear friends have not left Naples without saying adieu to their old, but most attached friend. No, I thought your statement could not be correct; and yet it agitated me more than anything ought to agitate one who must so soon bid an eternal farewell to all that is dear to him."

It appeared that one of the persons present, had in passing, the *Grande Bretagne*, seen our carriages drawn out; and the courier busy in arranging them for our journey. The dear archbishop, mentioning his regret for our approaching departure, and the sadness with which he looked forward to our parting adieu, this person said, that he believed his reverend friend would be spared that pain, for some hours previously he had seen the carriages ready to convey us away. This intelligence so grieved the good Capecelatro, that it occasioned the tears I found still streaming down his pale and venerable face, which furnished such a proof of his affection as greatly moved me.

Every word he uttered was listened to as are the words of the dying, for we cannot hope to see him more. There was a solemnity mingled in the tenderness of his parting words, that I can never forget; and which even now, bring the warm drops of affection to my eyes. The dear, the estimable Ricciardis too, I seem still to hear their kind words, and to feel their tears on my cheek. And all this occurred but so few hours ago; and *now*, I have left those dear and attached friends, and sunny Naples, most probably for ever. Piazzi, the gifted and good – Monticelli, the sage and gentle – Salvaggi, the brilliant and well-read – Rocco Romano too, the brave and chivalrous Rocco Romano; Filangieri, the worthy son of a noble sire; Pepe, generous as courteous, and high-couraged; Ischitella, honest and frank – Cazarano, gay, and joyous as his clime; Puoti, accomplished and amiable; and St.

Angelo,[1] ever obliging and kind. These, and others, with whom we had equally frequent intercourse during our residence at Naples, all seem again to surround us, as in the last days we spent there, with warm expressions of attachment on their lips; and as warm regret at our departure, expressed in their countenances.

[1] Marchese Niccola Santangelo, later Minister of the Interior.

Appendices

Index

Appendix a: Lady Blessington

Lady Blessington was born on 1 September 1789 in the village of Knockbrit, near Cashel in county Tipperary. She was christened Margaret, known to her family as Sally and assumed the name of Marguerite on her marriage to the Earl of Blessington. Her father, Edmund Power, and her mother, Ellen Sheehy, were both of old Catholic stock and small land-owning families. Margaret Power was the second daughter and the fourth of seven children. As a child she was plain and delicate and somewhat of an ugly duckling among her lively brothers and sisters. Her childhood was not a happy one, chiefly due to the cruel, inhuman, selfish and thoroughly unsatisfactory character of her father. As Madden says, Edmund Power "became a ruined man, bankrupt in fortune, character and domestic happiness".

In 1804 at the age of 15 Margaret was forced into marriage with Captain Maurice St. Leger Farmer, an officer of the 47th Regiment of Foot, whose sadistic behaviour made a lasting impression on her mind and for the rest of her life, "although she grew in loveliness, she never provoked real passion nor sought to provoke it because her sexual sensibility was dead". After only three months with Farmer her sufferings became insupportable and she fled back to her family. For the next 3 years she lived miserably with her parents, but sometime in 1806 or 1807 she became acquainted with Captain Thomas Jenkins of the 11th Dragoons who had an estate in Hampshire. By this time her father's career was coming to its disastrous climax, and his revengeful, cruel and violent attitude towards Margaret caused her such unhappiness that she left home and went to Jenkins. It is thought that they first settled in Dublin, but by the autumn of 1809, Margaret Farmer now just 20 years old, was apparently established in Jenkins's house in Hampshire where she lived quietly for the next 5 years – whatever her relations were with Jenkins, and they were most likely more a liaison of convenience than one of passion, it was here in these peaceful surroundings that her true character blossomed and she gradually developed a brilliance and charm of conversation, a gift of putting others at their ease and inviting their confidence, which remained her outstanding characteristics and were her success as hostess and ruler of a salon. At all events when she and Jenkins eventually came to live in London, Margaret Farmer emerged as one of the most widely read and best informed persons in London Society. She first met Charles John Gardiner, then Viscount Mountjoy, in 1816 when Jenkins brought him to their house; later Jenkins and Margaret stayed with him at Mountjoy Forest in Ireland. Later in that year Lord Mountjoy was created Earl of Blessington and shortly afterwards he seems to have intimated to Jenkins that he considered Mrs. Farmer the ideal person to become the Countess of Blessington (Lord Blessington had already had a mistress whom he had later married but she was now dead). However, since Captain Farmer was still alive, it was obvious that no marriage could take place. Lord Blessington thereupon made Jenkins the audacious offer of ten thousand pounds if he would relinquish Margaret. Nothing seems known of her reactions to this proposal, but she was soon installed in a house in Manchester Square by Lord Blessington who behaved with great correctness and never saw her alone. As Sadleir points out this is further evidence of the "sexual nullity" of Margaret Farmer. On 21 October 1817 Captain Farmer fell to his death from a window in the King's Bench after a drunken party, and on 16 February 1818, at the Church in Bryanston Square, Margaret Farmer became Marguerite, Countess of Blessington.

After a honeymoon in Ireland, the Earl and Countess of Blessington took up residence at No. 11 St. James's Square which was "fitted up like the palace of a Sybarite", and where in spite of her past history and the slights she had to endure from the aristocratic hostesses of London society, she soon established a salon which was known for its distinguished conversation and which was visited by all the notabilities in the political, literary and artistic life of London.

It was to this salon one evening in the autumn of 1821 that Count Alfred d'Orsay was brought by his brother-in-law, the Duc de Guiche, and thus began the remarkable friendship between the Blessingtons and Count d'Orsay. At that time Gillion Gaspare Alfred de Grimaud, Comte d'Orsay et du Saint Empire was 20 years old, Lady Blessington was 32 and Lord Blessington 7 years her senior.

On 25 August of the following year, Lord and Lady Blessington, accompanied by Lady Blessington's youngest sister, Mary Ann Power (who married Baron de Marsault in 1832), left London for Paris, and on 12 September, together with a host of retainers, they set off on their long continental tour. Their lumbering cavalcade of several carriages, piled high with every kind of luxurious equipment considered necessary for the comfort of travellers, caused so much commotion in the streets of Paris that it is reported one of the onlookers thought a regiment was setting out for war.

The cavalcade spent a week in Geneva, a few days in Berne, Zurich and Lucerne; then back to Geneva, to Lyons, and on 17 October they arrived at Vienne where they spent 3 weeks. On 9 November they moved on to Grenoble, St. Marcellin, Valence, Montélimar, Orange, and were at Avignon on the 20th where they stayed 3 months. It was here that Count d'Orsay, having resigned his commission in the French army, was invited to join them and from then onwards he became a member of their household. They left Avignon on 16 February travelling via Aix-en-Provence, Marseilles, Toulon, Fréjus, Cannes and Nice (where they spent 2 weeks), to Mentone, Ventimiglia, Oneglia, Noli and Voltri; finally 6 months after leaving London they reached Genoa on 13 March. Here they made the acquaintance of Byron, and Lady Blessington's remarkable book, *Conversations of Lord Byron with the Countess of Blessington*, not only provides us with a detailed account of their association but reveals the genuine intelligence of Lady Blessington and her undoubted powers of fascination. Leaving Genoa on 3 June, they reached Lucca 3 days later and arrived at Florence on 8 June where they stayed 3 weeks. From Florence they went via Siena, Radicofani and Orvieto to Rome for a week's stay. Finally, after passing through Terracina, they arrived at Naples on 17 July 1823.

The two and a half years that Lady Blessington spent at Naples must have been the happiest time of her life. Here she is revealed as astonishingly beautiful and witty, and "endowed with rare mental qualities and rare gifts and graces". Madden writes of her salon at Naples as "gay, enlivening, of cheerful character, and abounding in drollery and good-humour . . . Seldom, I think, did an Englishwoman abroad surround herself with such a company of *savants*. Always accompanied by an erudite *cicerone* when visiting places of historic or antiquarian interest". Of her character, he writes, "Greatness and magnificence were not thrust upon her – she seemed born to them. In all positions she had the great art of being perfectly at home. There was a naturalness in her demeanour, a grace and gentleness in her mind and manner – a certain kindliness of disposition and absence of all affection – a noble frankness about her, which left her in all circles at her ease – sure of pleasing, and easily amused by agreeable and clever people."

The household at Naples consisted of Lord and Lady Blessington, Miss Mary Ann Power, Count d'Orsay and, for part of the time, Charles James Mathews, the young architect whom Lord Blessington had engaged for his property in Ireland.

Lady Blessington's apparently sudden departure from Naples is not explained in her journals, but Madden quotes some anonymous verses addressed to her on leaving Naples "in consequence of the climate injuring her health."

On leaving Naples in February 1826, the Blessington household went to Rome for 3 weeks and arrived in Florence in March where they stayed for 9 months. Lord Blessington's health began to give trouble and they agreed to go to Genoa for a few weeks, but then decided to go back to Pisa where Count d'Orsay's sister and her husband, the Duc and Duchess de Guiche, were then living. After 4 months in Pisa, Lady Blessington heard that her old friend, Walter Savage Landor, had been taken ill at Florence and they decided to return there. It was while in Florence that the monstrous idea of a marriage between Count d'Orsay and Lady Harriet Gardiner, Lord Blessington's only surviving legitimate child, was conceived, and Lady Harriet, now barely 15 years old, was brought to Florence from Ireland. The English community at Florence was so affronted by this proposal that the Blessington party left via Rome for Naples where the marriage took place. Immediately afterwards they all went to Rome where they stayed until May 1828 when they began their homeward journey. Travelling via Ravenna, Ferrara, Padua, Venice (here they stayed a few weeks), Vicenza, Verona, Milan, Bologna, Modena, Parma, Piacenza, Genoa (where they caught sight of Byron's daughter, Ada), they crossed the frontier into France.They travelled along the Riviera to Marseilles, through Provence to Lyons and finally arrived at Paris where they set up their own establishment.

On 23 May Lord Blessington fell seriously ill and died two days later.

I think it not inappropriate here to comment on what Henry Fox has to say in his Journal,[1] since he refers constantly to the Blessingtons and usually in most unfavourable terms. Although when Fox was staying at Naples he fell under the spell of d'Orsay and at that time writes of him most extravagantly, he changes his mind about Lady Blessington who took him into the Villa Gallo at Naples and nursed him for nearly two months after an accident. His mother, Lady Holland, writing to him on 9 May 1828 says, "I have had a goodwill to Lady Blessington ever since she lodged, tended and nursed you so kindly when you had your fall; and you then, I thought, praised her and d'Orsay for qualities beyond their deserts – He was not esteemed in this country at all."[2] However, later at Rome and after the scandalous marriage of d'Orsay with Lord Blessington's daughter, Fox reverts to reviling that ménage. "They were dressed gorgeously as Turks. But Lady Blessington looked like one of her profession", he remarks when describing the appearance of Lord and Lady Blessington at a ball given by the French Ambassador at Rome in January 1827. In fact, his Journal is more often than not filled with most disagreeable and malicious aspersions on the people of whom he writes. At one time he is the bosom friend of Lady Westmorland, but ends by saying how scandalous her behaviour is and sends back her letters unopened. He makes scathing remarks about Sir William Gell who "never did a bad turn to anyone, gossip though he was". Fox left England because he was on bad terms with his family and constantly refers to them in most disagreeable terms but later writes of his "tender affection" for them. His devotion to his friend Edward Cheyney was extreme, yet in the end he broke off this friendship and blamed Cheyney for dragging him into the "silly business" about d'Orsay's libel on Lady Westmorland and made him "quarrel with him and many of his other friends". He ends by saying that Cheyney was "the worst counsellor I ever knew". Fox's own life was far from being beyond reproach. For instance he related in considerable detail how he became the lover of Teresa Guiccoli, the former mistress of Byron. At first he

[1] *Journal of The Hon. Henry Edward Fox 1818–1830*, edited by The Earl of Ilchester. London, Butterworth, 1923.

[2] *Elizabeth Lady Holland to her Son 1821–1845*, edited by The Earl of Ilchester. London, John Murray, 1946, p. 84.

writes of her in a most crude and coarse manner but ends by eulogies of praise. His views in general are those of one young and brash, Marchesa Iris Origo remarks in *The Last Attachment* he was "a beautiful and charming cad" and Archbishop David Mathew in his book, *Lord Acton, The Formative Years*, refers to "the little delicate bitter Henry Fox". His opinions would appear to change according to what company he was keeping at the time and who or what was fashionable in those circles. It is, however, a remarkable fact that in spite of Fox's abuse of the Blessingtons he continued to dine with them and visit them constantly.

Lady Blessington stayed on in Paris, but now the scandal, unjustified as it probably was, relating to her and to Count d'Orsay began to rear its ugly head. Lady Blessington was genuinely overwhelmed by her husband's death and herself fell ill for a time. Thereafter her whole personality seemed to change – she was quieter, more serious; her merry laughter, carefree airs and lively vivacity became Neapolitan memories. Calamity had begun its fateful walk, although the real blow to her heart was to come in 1831 when she was to write in her "Night Book", "We make temples in our hearts, in which we worship an idol, until we discover the object of our love was a false god; and then it is not the idol only that is destroyed – the shrine is ruined." D'Orsay continued to reside with his wife and mother-in-law and they all remained in Paris throughout the Revolution of 1830. In November they finally returned to London where Lady Blessington sub-let her house in St. James's Square and rented that of Lord Mountford in Seamore Place, Park Lane.

At the time of Count d'Orsay's marriage to Lady Harriet Gardiner, Lady Blessington had stipulated that Lady Harriet be left alone by her husband for the first 4 years of their marriage, but she failed to foresee the scandal that would link her own name with that of d'Orsay and which would assume a particularly disagreeable character when he was actually married to Lord Blessington's daughter. It seems almost unbelievable, but some time before the marriage Lord Blessington had offered to re-arrange his will in such a way that Count d'Orsay would be provided with a fortune if he married one of Lord Blessington's daughters. It is not my intention to describe in any detail the complexities of this will, the ensuing law suits or the wicked perfidy of d'Orsay, who "in his wild greed for money attempted the ruin both of his wife and benefactress." His despicable behaviour was to break Lady Blessington's heart. Nor do I propose to enter into the financial difficulties which beset Lady Blessington after her return to England until the end of her life. All this has been set down in detail in the works I have cited in the *Preface*. Suffice it to say that on Lady Blessington's return to England, she found herself left only with her jointure of £2,000 a year and the unexpired portion of the lease of the house in St. James's Square. She would have naturally assumed that Count and Countess d'Orsay, who were living as part of her household, would inherit large sums by the will of her husband, but she did not foresee the break up of the marriage, the challenging of the will by Lord Blessington's illegitimate son, Charles John Stewart Gardiner, or the reckless and wanton extravagance over the future years of d'Orsay.

During the second half of 1831 Countess d'Orsay fled from Seamore Place and took refuge with her Gardiner relatives. Count d'Orsay remained with Lady Blessington. Although later on when she moved to Gore House and he was beset by creditors, he lived in a small house next door, but to all intents and purposes d'Orsay was considered as one of Lady Blessington's household. This second half of 1831 is very important in the life of Lady Blessington but little is known about it.

In spite of all trials, scandal and ignominy. Lady Blessington remained outwardly loyal to Count d'Orsay; also to the impoverished members of her own family whom she felt bound to assist. To these ends she set herself to make money by writing the books, poems, and innumerable articles which were to occupy the greater part of each day for the rest of her life. On 22 October we find Sir William Gell writing to her, "I am delighted to see that the spirit of order which you always possessed, and which has done so much good on other occasions, has enabled you to take care of such of your friends as have less foresight than yourself. My preaching has the peculiar advantage of coming from a person who is always in debt and always in the last stage of poverty himself." What this effort must have meant to Lady Blessington can be described in her own words, "great trials require great courage, and all our energy is called up to enable us to bear them. But it is the minor cares of life that wear out the body, because, singly and in detail, they do not appear sufficiently important to oblige us to rally our forces and spirits to support them. Many minds that have withstood severe trials have been broken down by a succession of ignoble cares." However, in 1833, Tom Moore found her one evening "in her gay rooms splendidly lighted up and herself in a similar state of illumination sitting 'alone in her glory' reading. It was like the solitude of some princess confined in a fairy palace."

Lady Blessington lived at Seamore Place for 5 years, but in 1833 her house was broken into and she suffered the severe loss of her plate and jewellery. This made it all the more necessary for her to augment her income and hence-forward she worked long hours a day at her desk developing into a popular and fashionable writer. Early in 1836 she moved to Gore House, Kensington where, as at Seamore Place, she continued to receive in her salon the most distinguished men of intellect of the day. From 1843 troubles and afflictions beset her to an even greater extent and her health began to suffer. Count d'Orsay grew more and more reckless, deceitful and extravagant – debts piled up and no amount of industry on the part of Lady Blessington could produce enough money to meet them. By 1846 clamorous debtors made it clear that a crash was approaching. The disaster came on 7 May 1849, when on that day, and twelve subsequent days, the sale of Gore House and practically all of her possessions were sold. The sale realised about £12,000: this and her jointure of £2,000 was all that was available to settle the creditors.

Lady Blessington left London accompanied by her two nieces a fortnight before the sale took place and arrived at Paris in the middle of April, Count d'Orsay having fled there two weeks earlier. This appalling disaster was too much for Lady Blessington, and on 4 June 1849 she was suddenly taken ill with acute heart trouble, rendered unconscious and died almost immediately. She was buried in a mausoleum of granite in the shape of a pyramid in the hillside cemetery of Chambourcy near St. Germain-en-Laye. Count d'Orsay, who died on 4 August 1852, was interred there beside her.

Something must be said about the relationship between Lady Blessington and Count d'Orsay. As has been remarked elsewhere the terrible experience of her first marriage made its physical aspects abhorrent to her and there is no evidence that thereafter she took any personal interest in sex or wish for it. She was undoubtedly devoted to Count d'Orsay, but this seems more in the nature of a mother's love. As so often is the case, the more dishonourable and wicked the conduct of the child, the greater grows the mother's desire to protect and defend; this perhaps explains why d'Orsay remained a member of her household to the end and why she worked herself to death to pay their debts. Count d'Orsay, that handsome, artistically-gifted but vain and frivolous young man must in some manner have loved Lady Blessington, but his reckless extravagance, his irresponsible and reprehensible behaviour undoubtedly broke her heart. It is significant that when the Neapolitan journals came to be published no mention is made of Count d'Orsay. Perhaps the thought of those happy days was too poignant. Their long and close association never ceased to give rise to scandalous talk. The world thought they were lovers when they were alive and the world continued to think so long after they were dead, but Henry Fox writing in his *Journal* (p. 281) says that Lord Blessington confided to him that Lady Blessington had a spinal complaint which prevented him from exercising his matrimonial duties and Michael Sadleir in *Blessington-d'Orsay* has put forward the convincing theory that d'Orsay was impotent. If this was so, all is said on the subject; and we must bear in mind that three years after Lady Blessington's death, Madden visited d'Orsay in Paris. "In losing her", he said, "I have lost everything in this world. She was to me a mother, a dear, dear mother, a true loving mother!" The tragedy of Lady Blessington's life cannot be better expressed than in the words of Michael Sadleir:

Through the gilded but unhappy years which were the rest of her life, the soul of Lady Blessington was dead. In childhood half her nature had been paralysed by a man's brutal lust, the other half, late in the year 1831, was killed by the baseness of a mere trousered exquisite.[1]

[1] Sadleir, *op cit*, pp. 356, 191.

Appendix b: Poems

To Pompeii

Lonely City of the Dead!
Body, whence the Soul has fled,
Leaving still upon thy face
Such a mild and pensive grace,
As the lately dead display
While yet stamped upon frail clay,
Rests the impress of the mind,
That the fragile earth refined.

Let me question thee of those
Who within thy depths repose,
Those whose eyes like mine, have dwelt
On these scenes – whose hearts have felt
All that human hearts must know,
In a world where joy and woe
Chase each other – 'tis the doom
From the cradle to the tomb.

Tell me when the skies did lower,
Darken'd by the lurid shower,
That yon mountain in made ire
Scatter'd forth 'midst smoke and fire;
Did *they* dread the hand of Fate
Knocking at the City's gate?
Did *they* deem that Death was nigh
As they eyed the threat'ning sky?

Did the mother closer press
Her sleeping babe, and trembling bless
Its slumbers, nestling to its sire,
He, who vainly would inspire

Hopes he could no longer feel,
While his words amid each peal
Of thunder loud reach'd not the ear,
And more frantic grew her fear?

Did the bridegroom seek his bride,
Draw her wildly to his side,
Clasping her to his fond heart,
Swearing Death ev'n should not part
Souls so linked, then madly dare
Through the dense crowd her form to bear,
Till the burning show'rs that fall
O'er them close, like funeral pall?

Did the miser seek his gold,
And within his garments' fold
Hug the treasure loved too well,
Treasure which, like potent spell,
Drew him back (though Death unfurl'd)
His dark flag and ruin hurl'd
To some deep and secret cave,
Once his coffer – now his grave?

And ye walls, with pictures dight,
For long ages shut from light –
Ye, upon whose colours gay
Glad eyes dwelt each happy day,
Eyes, that on you look'd their last
Ere the hour of death was past,
Did ye echo to the wail
That had made stern hearts to quail?

But ye answer not – yet speech
Graver lesson could not teach
Than your silence, as alone,
Rapt, I hear the dying moan
Of the zephyr, while its sigh
Waves the vine in passing by,
Every soft and gentle breath
Seeming requiem of death.

Farewell! City of the Dead!
O'er whom centuries have fled,
Leaving on your buried face
Not one mark Time loves to trace;
Dumb as Egypt's corses, you
Strangely meet our anxious view,
Showing to the eager gaze
But cold, still shades of ancient days.

Lines on the Death of Lord Byron

(a)

And art thou fled – and is that mind subdued?
That glorious mind, by Genius' self imbued;
Whose bright effusions, free from tame control,
Struck with deep sympathy each general soul.
And is that hand benumb'd which struck the lyre
With all the fervour of poetic fire,
And sent forth strains that wrung the trembling heart
With feelings thou alone couldst e'er impart?
Alas! the hand's unnerved! – the strain is o'er,
And Britain's noblest poet we deplore.
The narrow grave contains what rests of thee,
Who gave thy life to Greece and Liberty –
But though thy mighty spirit hence has fled,
And thou art number'd with the silent dead,
As cold and passionless as meaner clay,
That ne'er had glowed with inspiration's ray,
Thy name shall live, inscribed in Albion's page,
The pride and boast of many a future age:
And pilgrims journeying from each distant land
shall seek thy grave, and o'er it pensive stand
To read that name, to every nation known,
And dear to each, as if thou wert her own;
While Freedom with the Muse shall o'er thy bier
Entwine their wreaths, embalm'd by many a tear.

(*b*)

In gilded halls where crowds surround,
  And all are gay, or seem to be,
I shrink from Music's joyous sound,
  And pensive Memory strays to thee.

I think upon that lofty brow,
  Which I again shall never see,
That in the grave is mouldering now,
  And scarce retains a trace of thee.

I think upon those dark gray eyes
  Through which the soul shone out, and see
No tint save twilight's soften'd skies
  That brings their colour back to me.

I think upon that scornful mouth
  That rarely smiled, yet smiled with me;
Like summer lightnings in the south
  That smile appear'd, then fled from thee.

I think upon that glorious mind
  Inspired by Genius, and can see
Byron no poet left behind
  To fire or melt the soul like thee.

Index of
Persons and Places